Samsung® Galaxy Tabs

FOR

DUMMIES®

A Wiley Brand

Portable Edition

by Dan Gookin

FOR

DUMMIES®
A Wiley Brand

Samsung® Galaxy Tabs For Dummies®, Portable Edition
Published by
John Wiley & Sons, Inc.
111 River Street, Hoboken,
NJ 07030-5774
www.wiley.com

Contents at a Glance

Contents

Introduction

*I*t's not a cell phone. It's not a computer. It's the latest craze: the tablet. It exists somewhere between the traditional computer and the newfangled smart phone. That makes the tablet kind of an oddball, but quite a popular oddball.

The Galaxy Tab is Samsung's solution to your mobile, wireless, communications, information, and entertainment needs. Oh, I could blather on and on about how wonderful it is, but my point is simple: The Galaxy Tab does so much, and yet it comes with very scant documentation. If you want more information about how to get the most from the Galaxy Tab, you need another source. This little book is that source.

About This Book

This book was written to help you get the most from the Galaxy Tab's massive potential. It's a reference. Each chapter covers a specific topic, and the sections within each chapter address an issue related to the topic. The idea is to show you how things are done on the Galaxy Tab to help you get the most out of it without overwhelming you with information.

You have nothing to memorize, no sacred utterances or animal sacrifices, and definitely no PowerPoint presentations. Instead, every section explains a topic as though it's the first thing you read in this book. Nothing is assumed, and everything is cross-referenced. The idea here isn't to learn anything. This book's philosophy is to help you look it up, figure it out, and get on with your life.

How to Use This Book

This book follows a few conventions for using the Galaxy Tab. First of all, the Galaxy Tab is referred to as the *Galaxy Tab* throughout the book. I might also break down and call it the

Tab for short, just because, for some reason, typing the word *Galaxy* isn't the easiest thing for me.

The way you interact with the Galaxy Tab is by using its *touchscreen,* the glassy part of the device as it's facing you. The device also has some physical buttons, as well as some holes and connectors. All those items are described in Chapter 1.

There are various ways to touch the screen, which are explained and named in Chapter 3.

Chapter 4 discusses text input on the Galaxy Tab, which involves using an onscreen keyboard. You can also input text by speaking to the Galaxy Tab, which is also covered in Chapter 4.

Foolish Assumptions

Even though this book is written with the gentle hand-holding required by anyone who is just starting out, or who is easily intimidated, I've made a few assumptions. For example, I assume that you're a human being and not the emperor of Jupiter.

My biggest assumption: You have a Samsung Galaxy Tab of your own. Though you could use this book without owning a Galaxy Tab, I think the people in the Phone Store would grow tired of you reading it while standing in front of the demo model.

There is more than one Galaxy Tab gizmo available. This book covers both the cellular data and Wi-Fi versions. The Wi-Fi Galaxy Tab uses standard computer wireless networking to communicate with the Internet. I call it the Wi-Fi Tab. The Galaxy Tab that uses the digital cellular network to communicate with the Internet, as well as Wi-Fi, I refer to as the cellular Galaxy Tab.

Only a few subtle differences between the Wi-Fi and cellular Galaxy Tabs exist, and those are noted in the text. Otherwise, whenever I write Galaxy Tab or Tab, the text refers to both models.

I also assume that you have a computer, either a desktop or laptop. The computer can be a PC or Windows computer or a Macintosh. Oh, I suppose it could also be a Linux computer. In any event, I refer to your computer as "your computer" throughout this book. When directions are specific to a PC or Mac, the book says so.

Programs that run on the Galaxy Tab are *apps,* which is short for *applications.* A single program is an app.

Finally, this book doesn't assume that you have a Google account, but already having one helps. Information is provided in Chapter 2 about setting up a Google account — an extremely important part of using the Galaxy Tab. Having a Google account opens up a slew of useful features, information, and programs that make using your Tab more productive.

Icons Used in This Book

This icon flags useful, helpful tips or shortcuts.

This icon marks a friendly reminder to do something.

This icon marks a friendly reminder not to do something.

This icon alerts you to overly nerdy information and technical discussions of the topic at hand. Reading the information is optional, though it may win you the Daily Double on *Jeopardy!*

Where to Go from Here

Start reading! Observe the table of contents and find something that interests you. Or, look up your puzzle in the index. When those suggestions don't cut it, just start reading Chapter 1.

My e-mail address is dgookin@wambooli.com. Yes, that's my real address. I reply to all e-mail I get, and you'll get a quick reply if you keep your question short and specific to this book. Although I do enjoy saying "Hi," I cannot answer technical support questions, resolve billing issues, or help you troubleshoot your Galaxy Tab. Thanks for understanding.

You can also visit my web page for more information or as a diversion: www.wambooli.com.

Enjoy this book and your Galaxy Tab!

1

Welcome to Tablet Land

. . . .

In This Chapter

▶ Unboxing your Galaxy Tab

▶ Charging the battery

▶ Locating important things

▶ Working with the MicroSD card

▶ Getting optional accessories

. . . .

I thoroughly enjoy getting a new gizmo and opening its box. Expectations build. Joy is released. Then frustration descends like a grand piano pushed out a third-story window. That's because any new electronic device, especially something as sophisticated as the Galaxy Tab, requires a bit of hand-holding. There's a lot of ground to cover, but it all starts with opening the box and with reading this gentle introduction to the Samsung Galaxy Tab.

Set Up Your Galaxy Tab

Odds are good that the folks who sold you the Galaxy Tab have already done some preconfiguration. In the United States, the Tab is available primarily from cellular phone providers, and getting digital cellular service is a usual part of purchasing the Tab.

If you have a cellular (non–Wi-Fi) Tab, it's most likely been unboxed and completely manhandled by the Phone Store people — maybe even in front of your own eyes! That's a necessary step for a 4G Tab, and even though it might have broken your heart (as it did mine), you need that initial setup done before you can unbox and set up the Galaxy Tab for yourself.

- ✐ If you ordered your Galaxy Tab online, the setup may have been done before the Tab shipped. If not, see Chapter 2.

- ✐ The initial setup identifies the Tab with the cellular network, giving it a network ID and associating the ID with your cellular bill.

- ✐ The Wi-Fi Tab doesn't require setup with a cellular provider, but it does require a Wi-Fi signal to use many features. See Chapter 10 for information on configuring your Tab for use with a Wi-Fi network.

- ✐ Additional software setup is required for the Tab, primarily to link it with your Gmail and other Google accounts on the Internet. See Chapter 2 for the details.

Opening the box

The Galaxy Tab fits snugly inside its box. You'll find it lying right on top. Remove the device by locating and lifting a cardboard tab at the side of the box. After liberating your Galaxy Tab, remove the plastic sheet that's clinging to the device's front and back.

In the box's bottom compartment, you may find

- ✐ **A USB cable:** You can use it to connect the Tab to a computer or a wall charger.

- ✐ **A wall charger:** It comes in two pieces. The larger piece has the USB connector, and the smaller piece is customized for your locality's wall sockets.

- ✐ **Earbud-style earphones:** The Tab may have come with a set of earphones for listening to music and other media in the privacy of your own head.

- ✐ **Pamphlets with warnings and warranty information:** You also receive the brief *Master Your Device* booklet, which you're free to ignore because, honestly, this book puts that thing to shame.

- ✐ **A Gift Certificate for the Media Hub:** If you're lucky, you might find a $25 gift certificate for the Samsung Media Hub app. Do not throw it away!

✔ **The 4G SIM card holder:** For the cellular Tab, you'll need a 4G SIM card. The Phone Store people may have tossed its credit card–sized holder into the box as well. You can throw it out.

Go ahead and free the USB cable and power charger from their clear plastic cocoons. Assemble the power charger's two pieces, which fit so snugly together that you'll probably never be able to pry them apart.

Keep the box for as long as you own your Galaxy Tab. If you ever need to return the thing or ship it somewhere, the original box is the ideal container. You can shove the pamphlets and papers back into the box as well.

Charging the battery

The first thing that I recommend you do with your Galaxy Tab is give it a full charge. Obey these steps:

1. **Assemble the wall adapter that came with the Tab.**

2. **Attach the USB cable to the Galaxy Tab.**

    The side of the cable end that's labeled *Samsung* faces you as you're looking at the front of the Tab.

3. **Attach the other end of the USB cable to the wall adapter.**

4. **Plug the wall adapter into the wall.**

Upon success, you may see a large Battery icon appear on the Galaxy Tab touchscreen. The icon gives you an idea of the current battery-power level and lets you know that the Galaxy Tab is functioning properly, though you shouldn't be alarmed if the Battery icon fails to appear.

✔ Your Galaxy Tab most likely came partially charged from the factory, though I still recommend giving it an initial charge just in case, as well as to familiarize yourself with the process.

✔ The USB cable is used for charging the Galaxy Tab and for connecting it to a computer to share information or exchange files or use the Galaxy Tab as a computer modem. (You find out about this *tethering* process in Chapter 10.)

✏ You can also charge the Tab by connecting it to a computer's USB port. As long as the computer is on, the Tab charges.

✏ The battery charges more efficiently if you plug it into a wall rather than charge it from a computer's USB port.

✏ The Galaxy Tab does not feature a removable battery.

Know Your Way Around the Galaxy

"Second star to the right and straight on till morning" may get Peter Pan to Neverland, but for navigating your way around the Galaxy Tab, you need more-specific directions.

Finding things on the Tab

Take heed of Figure 1-1, which is my attempt at illustrating generic Galaxy Tab hardware features. Follow along on your own Tab as you find key features, described in this section. Keep in mind that the features shown in Figure 1-1 may not be in the exact same spot on your Tab.

Dock/USB power connector: The key to discovering things on your Tab is to first find the Power/USB jack, as shown in Figure 1-1. It's a thin slot located on the bottom side of the Tab, or the side I call the bottom. Because the Tab has no buttons or other easily identifiable marks on its front, locating the Power/USB jack first helps you orient the Tab as well as locate other goodies, which are illustrated in the figure. The slot is also where the Tab connects to the dock, if you have one.

Touchscreen display: The biggest part of the Tab is its touchscreen display, which occupies almost all the territory on the front of the device. The touchscreen display is a see-touch thing: You look at it and also touch it with your fingers to control the Tab.

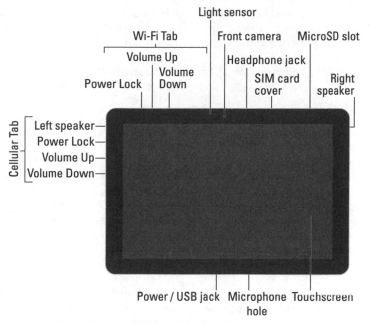

Light sensor

Wi-Fi Tab   Front camera   MicroSD slot

Volume Up   Headphone jack

Volume   SIM card   Right
Power Lock   Down   cover   speaker

Cellular Tab

Left speaker—
Power Lock—
Volume Up—
Volume Down—

Power / USB jack   Microphone   Touchscreen
                   hole

Figure 1-1: Things on the Galaxy Tab.

Front camera: The Galaxy Tab's front-facing camera is centered above the touchscreen. The camera is used for taking self-portraits as well as for video conferencing.

Light sensor: Though it's difficult to see, just to the left of the front camera is a teensy light sensor. It's used to help adjust the brightness level of the touchscreen.

Around the Galaxy Tab, you find a variety of buttons, holes, connectors, and other doodads, all carefully explained here:

Headphone jack: Atop the Tab case, you see a hole where you can connect standard headphones.

MicroSD slot: The memory slot is where you'll find the Galaxy Tab's MicroSD card, a media card on which information is stored. See the next section.

SIM card cover: This spot is used to access the cellular Tab's SIM card, which is inserted into a slot beneath the cover.

Speaker(s): Stereo speakers are located on the left and right sides of the Tab. (Feel free to remove the plastic sticker beneath the right speaker if you find one there.)

Microphone: A tiny hole on the bottom of the Tab (see Figure 1-1) is where you find the device's microphone.

Volume Up/Volume Down: The Tab's volume control is located on the left side of the cellular unit, just below the Power Lock button. On the Wi-Fi Tab, the volume control is on top of the unit, as illustrated in Figure 1-1. The button toward the top of the unit is Volume Up, and the other button is Volume Down.

 Power Lock: The Power Lock button is labeled with the universal power icon, shown in the margin. Press this button to turn on the Tab, to lock it (put it to sleep), to wake it up, and to turn it off. Directions for performing these activities are found in Chapter 2.

Figure 1-2 illustrates the back of the Galaxy Tab. It's mostly boring except for the device's main camera, illustrated in the figure. In fact, the entire Tab is physically boring front and back; all the real goodies are found on its edges.

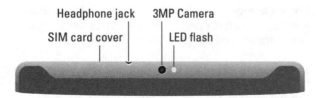

Headphone jack   3MP Camera

SIM card cover   LED flash

Figure 1-2: Galaxy Tab, upper back.

The back of the Galaxy Tab can be black or white, which is a choice you make when you buy the device. There is no internal difference between the black or white Tab.

✔ The Power Lock and Volume buttons are in different locations for the cellular and Wi-Fi Tab models.

✔ You'll rarely, if ever, access the SIM card.

 ✔ SIM stands for Subscriber Identity Module. The SIM card is used by your cellular provider to identify your Tab and keep track of the amount of data you access. Yep, that's so you can be billed properly. The SIM also gives your cellular Tab a phone number, though that number is merely an account and not something you can dial into or send a text message.

✔ Be careful not to confuse the SIM card hole and the removable storage media (MicroSD card) holes; they're not the same thing.

✔ Don't stick anything into the microphone hole. The only things you need to stick into the Tab are the USB cable (or the connector on the dock) or headphones.

Removing and inserting the MicroSD card

Some versions of the Galaxy Tab come with a media card, called a MicroSD card. It's used to store your stuff, similar to the way a media card stores images in a digital camera. The MicroSD card is basically a tiny, thumbnail-size storage device.

To remove the card, such as when you want to replace it with a higher-capacity card or to use it in some other device, follow these steps:

1. **Turn off your Galaxy Tab.**

   Specific directions are offered in Chapter 2, but for now press and hold the Power button (see Figure 1-1) and choose Power Off from the Device Options menu.

   If the Tab isn't turned off, you can damage the media card when you remove it.

   To ensure that the Tab is turned off, press and release the Power button quickly. The Tab shouldn't come back to life. If it does, then repeat Step 1.

2. **Open the teensy hatch that covers the MicroSD slot.**

3. **Use your fingernail to press the MicroSD card inward a tad.**

   The MicroSD card is spring-loaded, so pressing it in actually pops it out.

4. **Pinch the MicroSD card between your fingers and remove it completely.**

The MicroSD card is truly an itty-bitty thing, much smaller than your typical media card.

The Galaxy Tab still works without the MicroSD card installed. You won't be able to access any information that was stored on the card, which includes your contacts, pictures, videos, music, and other items necessary to use the Tab. So my advice is to keep the MicroSD card installed.

To insert a MicroSD card into your Galaxy Tab, follow these steps:

1. **Ensure that the Galaxy Tab is turned off.**

2. **Open the little hatch covering the MicroSD card slot.**

3. **Orient the MicroSD card so that the printed side is up and the teeny triangle on the card is pointing toward the Galaxy Tab.**

4. **Use your fingernail to gently shove the card all the way into the slot.**

   The card makes a faint clicking sound when it's fully inserted.

5. **Close the hatch covering the MicroSD card slot.**

After you install the card, turn on your Galaxy Tab by pressing and holding the Power button until the touchscreen comes to life.

- There are SD card adapters, into which you can insert a MicroSD card. The SD card adapter can then be used in any computer or digital device that reads SD cards.

- SD stands for *Secure Digital*. It is but one of about a zillion different media-card standards.

- MicroSD cards come in a smattering of capacities.

- In addition to the MicroSD card, the Galaxy Tab also features internal storage. That storage is used for the programs you install on the Tab, as well as for the Tab's operating system and other control programs. The internal storage is not used for your personal information, media, and other items, which is why it's necessary to keep the MicroSD card inside your Galaxy Tab.

Getting optional accessories

You can buy an assortment of handy Galaxy Tab accessories, and I'm sure that the pleasant people at the Phone Store showed you the variety when you bought your Tab. Here are just a few of the items that are available or that you can consider getting in order to complete your Tab experience:

Earphones: You can use any standard cell phone or portable media player earphones with the cellular Galaxy Tab. Simply plug the earphones into the headphone jack at the top of the Tab, and you're ready to go.

Cases: Various cases and case-stands are available for the Galaxy Tab. Some are mere enclosures, like a portfolio. Other cases can also be used as stands to prop up the Tab for easy viewing.

Keyboards: Several different types of keyboards are available for the Galaxy Tab, from the case-keyboard to keyboard docking stands or standard Bluetooth keyboards. They can both prop up the Tab for easy viewing as well as allow for faster typing than can be done on a touchscreen.

Multimedia Dock: The dock is merely a stand you can use to prop up the Tab for easy viewing. It has a speaker jack you can use to connect external speakers.

Galaxy Tab USB Adapter: This USB adapter isn't the same thing as the USB cable that came with your Tab. It's a dongle that plugs into the Tab's Power/USB jack that allows the Tab to host a USB device, such as a keyboard, mouse, modem, or external storage device (hard drive or optical drive).

HDMI adapter: The adapter plugs into the Power/USB jack. Into the adapter, you can plug an HDMI cable (which is extra) so that you can view the Tab's output on an HDMI-compatible monitor or television.

Screen protectors: These plastic, clingy things are affixed to the front of the Tab, right over the touchscreen. They help protect the touchscreen glass from finger smudges and sneeze globs while still allowing you to use the touchscreen.

Vehicle charger: You can charge the Galaxy Tab in your car when you buy the vehicle charger. This adapter plugs into your car's 12-volt power supply, in the receptacle once known as a cigarette lighter. The vehicle charger is a must-have if you plan to use the Galaxy Tab navigation features in your auto or you need a charge on the road.

Additional accessories may be available. Check the location where your Galaxy Tab was sold to inquire about new items.

2

The On and Off Chapter

. . . .

In This Chapter

▶ Setting up and configuring the Tab

▶ Unlocking the screen

▶ Waking the Galaxy Tab

▶ Getting a Google account

▶ Shutting down the Galaxy Tab

. . . .

1 remember reading my very first computer book, back during the steam-powered "microcomputer" era. The book had very clever and humorous directions for turning on the computer. When it came time to turn off the system, however, there was nothing. No information was written on the proper method for shutting down the computer. No details. No humor. Apparently you just turned off the beastie, either by thunking the big red switch or yanking the plug from the wall socket.

Things are better today, not only with technology but for technology books as well. This chapter not only shows you how to turn on the Galaxy Tab, but also offers directions on putting the thing to sleep *and* turning it off. As a bonus, there's some setup information tossed in as well. And, no, I didn't forget the humor.

Hello, Tab

In all the effort made by engineers and wizards to make technology easier, one area where they fail is in the basic way you turn on a gizmo. Take the Galaxy Tab: You have two different ways to turn it on, plus special bonus goodies happen the *first* time you turn on the Tab. This section discusses the details.

   ✔ Initial setup of the Galaxy Tab works best when you already have a Google, or Gmail, account on the Internet. If you lack a Google account, see the section "Setting up a Google account," later in this chapter, for details.

   ✔ Setup works differently depending on whether you have a cellular Tab or Wi-Fi only. When you have a Wi-Fi–only Tab, the cellular network activation stage is skipped during setup.

   ✔ See Chapter 10 for information on connecting your Galaxy Tab to a Wi-Fi network.

Turning on your Galaxy Tab (for the first time)

The very, very first time your Galaxy Tab was turned on was most likely at the Phone Store or at a factory if you ordered your Tab online. That process involved hooking up the Tab to the Phone Company's digital network, but that was the extent of the operation.

If the Phone Store hasn't configured your Tab, you have to do it. See the next section, "Activate your Galaxy Tab." Otherwise, skip ahead to the section "Your Google account."

Activate your Galaxy Tab

Follow these steps to turn on your Galaxy Tab for the first time and activate your cellular service:

   1. Press the Power Lock button.

You may have to press it longer than you think; when you see the Samsung Galaxy Tab logo appear on the screen, the Tab has started.

2. **Unlock the Tab by dragging your finger across the screen, as shown in Figure 2-1.**

   As you drag, an unlocking ring appears onscreen. Drag your finger until the padlock icon unlocks itself.

Touch the screen, then swipe to unlock

Figure 2-1: The main Galaxy Tab unlock screen.

Because you're starting the Tab for the first time, you see the initial screen for the setup program. The first thing to do is to tell the Tab which language to use.

3. **Choose English.**

4. **If you have a cellular Tab, follow these general substeps:**

   a. Touch the Activate button to activate your cellular account.

   b. Obey the directions given by your cellular provider.

   c. Keep reading in the next section, "Your Google account."

5. **If you have a Wi-Fi Tab, follow these general substeps:**

   a. Touch the Start button.

b. Choose a Wi-Fi network from the list displayed.

c. If prompted, use the onscreen keyboard to type in the Wi-Fi password.

d. Touch the Connect button.

e. Touch the Next button

f. Skip to Step 4 in the next section, "Your Google account."

After you activate the Tab, you see a Congratulations message. Touch the text Proceed with the Setup Process and continue reading with the next section.

If you have trouble activating the cellular Tab, contact your cellular provider. You need to read information from the Galaxy Tab's box, which has activation information printed on a label.

Your Google account

After your Galaxy Tab has been activated, the next step in configuring it is to synchronize the device with your Google account. Obey:

1. **Start the Galaxy Tab, if you haven't already.**

   Press the Power Lock button until you see the Samsung Galaxy Tab logo on the screen.

2. **If necessary, unlock the screen as described in the preceding section.**

3. **Choose your language and touch the Start button.**

4. **Ensure that there is a green check mark by the items listed on the Use Google's Location Service screen.**

   The two items help the Tab find itself on the Planet Earth. If the items aren't selected, touch the little square next to each item to place a green check mark there.

5. **Touch the Next button.**

6. **If prompted, enter the date and time.**

   Wi-Fi Tabs that aren't currently connected to a network need to have their time updated.

7. **Touch the Next button again.**

   It's time to set up your Google account.

8. **Touch the Email text box and type your Google account name.**

   Because you read the Tip icon at the start of this section, you've already set up and configured a Google account. Use the onscreen keyboard to type your Google account's e-mail address into the Email text box.

   If you haven't set up a Google account, see the section "Setting up a Google account," later in this chapter, for details.

   See Chapter 4 for more information about typing text on your Galaxy Tab.

9. **Touch the Password field and type your Google account password.**

10. **Touch the Sign In button.**

11. **Ensure that there are two green check marks for the items on the Backup and Restore screen.**

    With both check marks in place, the information on your Tab is synchronized with existing information in your Google account on the Internet. It's a good thing.

12. **Touch the Done button.**

The good news is that you're done. The better news is that you need to complete this setup only once on your Galaxy Tab. From this point on, starting the Tab works as described in the next few sections.

- The information synchronized on the Galaxy Tab includes the following items from your Google account on the Internet: the contact list, Gmail messages, calendar appointments, and other "Googly" information.

- One of the first things you may notice to be synchronized between your Tab and Google is your Gmail inbox. See Chapter 6 for more information on Gmail.

Turning on your Galaxy Tab

To turn on your Galaxy Tab, press and hold the Power Lock button. After a few seconds, you see the Samsung Galaxy Tab logo and then some hypnotic animation. The Tab is starting.

Eventually, you see the main unlock screen, shown earlier, in Figure 2-1. Use your finger to swipe the screen, as indicated in the figure. After your Galaxy Tab is unlocked, you can start using it — and, unlike the first time you turned the thing on, you aren't prompted to complete the setup routine (well, unless you skipped setup the first time).

You probably won't turn on your Galaxy Tab much in the future. Mostly, you'll unlock the gizmo. See the later section, "Unlocking the Tab."

Working the various lock screens

The unlock screen you see when you turn on or unlock the Tab isn't a tough lock to pick. In fact, it's known as the No Security option in the Set Lock Screen window. If you've added more security, you might see any one of three different lock screens.

The pattern lock, shown in Figure 2-2, requires that you trace your finger along a pattern that includes as many as nine dots on the screen. After you match the pattern, the Tab is unlocked, and you can start using it.

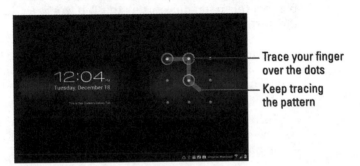

Trace your finger over the dots

Keep tracing the pattern

Figure 2-2: The Pattern Lock screen.

The PIN lock is shown in Figure 2-3. It requires that you input a secret number to unlock the Tab. Touch the OK button to accept input, or use the Del button to back up and erase.

Code turns to dots for added security

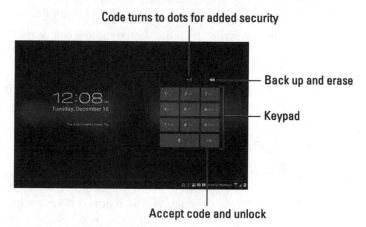

Back up and erase

Keypad

Accept code and unlock

Figure 2-3: The PIN Lock screen.

Finally, the password lock requires that you type a multi-character password on the screen before the Tab is unlocked. Touch the text box to see the onscreen keyboard and type the password, as shown in Figure 2-4. Touch the Done button to accept the password and unlock the Galaxy Tab.

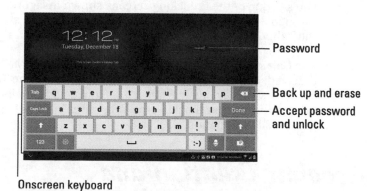

Password

Back up and erase

Accept password and unlock

Onscreen keyboard

Figure 2-4: The Password Lock screen.

Whether or not you see these various lock screens depends on how you've configured the Galaxy Tab's security.

- ✔ The pattern lock can start at any dot, not necessarily the upper-left dot, as shown earlier in Figure 2-2.

- ✔ The password lock must contain at least one letter and number, though it can also include a smattering of symbols and other characters.

- ✔ For additional information on working the onscreen keyboard, see Chapter 4.

Unlocking the Tab

You'll probably leave your Galaxy Tab on all the time. It was designed that way. The battery lasts quite a while, so when the Tab is bored or when you've ignored it for a while, it falls asleep. The Tab has locked itself, turning off the screen to save power.

You unlock the Galaxy Tab by pressing the Power Lock button. Unlike turning on the Tab, a quick press of the Power Lock button is all that's needed.

After unlocking the Tab, you see the unlock screen, shown in Figure 2-1. Or, if you've configured the Tab for more security, you see one of the unlocking screens shown in Figures 2-2 through 2-4. Simply unlock the screen, and you can start using the Tab.

The Galaxy Tab continues to run while it's locked. Mail is received, as are other notifications and updates. The Tab also continues to play music while it's sleeping, and the display is off. See the section "Locking the Tab," later in this chapter for additional information.

Account Creation and Configuration

After you've done the initial configuration as described earlier in this chapter, there's nothing else you need to do to set up the Galaxy Tab. If you've skipped that step or you need to create a Google account, follow the directions in this section to complete the setup process.

Setting up a Google account

To get the most from your Galaxy Tab, you must have a Google account. If you don't already have one, drop everything (but not this book) and follow these steps to obtain one:

1. **Open your computer's web browser program.**

   Yes, it works best if you use your computer, not the Tab, to complete these steps.

2. **Visit the main Google page at** `www.google.com`.

3. **Click the Sign In link.**

   Another page opens, and on it you can log in to your Google account, but you don't have a Google account, so:

4. **Click the link to create a new account.**

   The link is typically found beneath the text boxes where you would log in to your Google account. As I write this chapter, the link is titled Sign Up for a New Google Account.

5. **Continue heeding the directions until you've created your own Google account.**

Eventually, your account is set up and configured.

To try things out, log off from Google and then log back in. That way, you ensure that you've done everything properly — and remembered your password. (Your web browser may even prompt you to let it remember the password for you.)

I also recommend creating a bookmark for your account's Google page: The Ctrl+D or ⌘+D keyboard shortcut is used to create a bookmark in just about any web browser.

Continue reading in the next section for information on synchronizing your new Google account with the Galaxy Tab.

Attaching your Google account to the Galaxy Tab

Don't fret if you've failed to obey the prompts and neglected to sign in to your Google account when first configuring the Galaxy Tab. You can rerun the configuration setup at any time. Just follow these steps:

1. **Turn on or wake up the Galaxy Tab if it's not already on and eagerly awaiting your next move.**

2. **Unlock the Tab if necessary.**

   You can find directions earlier in this chapter, in the section "Working the various lock screens."

3. **Touch the Apps Menu button.**

   The Apps Menu button is located in the upper-right corner of the Home screen. Its icon is shown in the margin.

4. **Choose the Settings icon.**

   The Settings screen appears, which contains commands for configuring and setting options for the Galaxy Tab.

5. **Choose Accounts & Sync.**

6. **Touch the Add Account button in the upper-right part of the screen.**

7. **Choose Google.**

   At this point, you're signing into your Google account on the Galaxy Tab. Refer to the earlier section, "Your Google account," and start reading at Step 7.

Your goal is to synchronize your Google account information on the Internet with the information on your Galaxy Tab.

Adding your personal e-mail account to the Tab, as well as other free online e-mail accounts, is covered in Chapter 6.

Goodbye, Tab

I know of three ways to say goodbye to your Galaxy Tab, and only one of them involves training an elephant. The other two methods are documented in this section.

Locking the Tab

To lock the Tab, simply press its Power Lock button. The display goes dark; the Tab is locked. The Galaxy Tab still works while it's locked; it still receives e-mail, and can still play music. But it's not using as much power as it would with the display on.

Controlling the lock timeout

You can manually lock the Galaxy Tab at any time by pressing the Power Lock button. That's why it's called the Power *Lock* button. When you don't manually lock the Tab, it automatically locks itself after a given period of inactivity.

You have control over the automatic lock timeout value, which can be set anywhere from 15 seconds to one hour. Obey these steps:

1. **At the Home screen, touch the Apps Menu icon button.**

2. **Choose Settings.**

3. **Choose Display.**

4. **Choose Screen Timeout.**

5. **Choose a timeout value from the list.**

   I prefer 1 minute, which is also the standard value.

6. **Touch the Home icon button to return to the Home screen.**

The lock timer begins after a period of inactivity; when you don't touch the screen or tap an icon button, the timer starts ticking. About 5 seconds before the timeout value you set (refer to Step 5), the touchscreen dims. Then it turns off, and the Tab locks. If you touch the screen before then, the timer is reset.

Turning off the Galaxy Tab

To turn off the Tab, heed these steps:

1. **Press and hold the Power Lock button.**

   You see the Device Options menu, shown in Figure 2-5. (The Wi-Fi Tab's Device Options menu lacks a Restart command.)

Figure 2-5: The Device Options menu.

   If you chicken out and don't want to turn off the Tab, touch the Back icon button to dismiss the Device Options menu.

2. **Touch the Power Off item.**

3. **Touch OK.**

   The Galaxy Tab turns itself off.

The Tab doesn't run when it's off, so it doesn't remind you of appointments, collect e-mail, or let you hear any alarms you've set. The Tab also isn't angry with you for turning it off, though you may sense some resentment when you turn it on again.

3

Finding Your Way Around the Galaxy

• •

In This Chapter

▶ Working the touchscreen

▶ Changing the volume

▶ Getting around the Home screen

▶ Using icon buttons

▶ Running apps (programs)

▶ Checking notifications

▶ Finding all the apps

• •

I'm not certain, but I think the Galaxy Tab is more powerful than all the computers in the bat cave from the 1960s TV show, *Batman*. Those computers were impressive: They had lots of buttons and flashing lights. In today's high-tech world, however, sophisticated devices don't have a lot of buttons and flashing lights. In fact, the more sophisticated the device, such as your Galaxy Tab, the fewer the buttons and lights.

To accommodate for the lack of buttons, the Galaxy Tab features a touchscreen. You use the touchscreen to control the Tab, which is probably a new experience for you. To get you up to speed, and to get Batman up to speed should he be reading this book, I present this chapter on understanding the Galaxy Tab's touchscreen interface.

Basic Operations

It's not a computer. It's not a phone. The Galaxy Tab is truly something different, probably unlike anything you've ever used. To control this unique gizmo, you have to familiarize yourself with some basic tablet operations, as covered in this section.

Touching the touchscreen

Bereft of buttons and knobs, the way you control the Galaxy Tab is, for the most part, by manipulating things on the touchscreen with one or two fingers. It doesn't matter which fingers you use, and feel free to experiment with other body parts as well, though I find fingers to be handy.

You have specific ways to touch the touchscreen, and those specific ways have names. Here's the list:

Touch: The simplest way to manipulate the touchscreen is to touch it. You touch an object, an icon, a control, a menu item, a doodad, and so on. The touch operation is similar to a mouse click on a computer. It may also be referred to as a *tap* or *press*.

Double-tap: Touch the screen twice in the same location. Double-tapping can be used to zoom in on an image or a map, but it can also zoom out. Because of the double-tap's dual nature, I recommend using the pinch or spread operation instead when you want to zoom.

Long-press: A long-press occurs when you touch part of the screen and keep your finger down. Depending on what you're doing, a pop-up menu may appear, or the item you're long-pressing may get "picked up" so that you can move it around after a long-press. *Long-press* might also be referred to as *touch and hold* in some documentation.

Swipe: To swipe, you touch your finger on one spot and then drag it to another spot. Swipes can go up, down, left, or right, which moves the touchscreen content in the direction you swipe your finger. A swipe can be fast or slow. It's also called a *flick* or *slide*.

Pinch: A pinch involves two fingers, which start out separated and then are brought together. The effect is used to *zoom out,* to reduce the size of an image or see more of a map.

Spread: The opposite of pinch is spread. You start out with your fingers together and then spread them. The spread is used to *zoom in,* to enlarge an image or see more detail on a map.

Rotate: A few apps let you rotate an image on the screen by touching with two fingers and twisting them around a center point. Think of turning a combination lock on a safe, and you get the rotate operation.

Changing the orientation

The Galaxy Tab features a gizmo called an *accelerometer.* It determines in which direction the Tab is pointed or whether you've reoriented the device from an upright to a horizontal position, or even upside down. That way, the information on the Tab always appears upright, no matter how you hold it.

To demonstrate how the Galaxy Tab orients itself, rotate the Tab to the left or right. The Tab can be used in either vertical or horizontal orientations. Most apps change their orientation to match however you've turned the Tab.

The rotation feature may not work for all apps, especially Android apps designed for use on cell phones and not tablets. Some games present themselves in one orientation only.

  ✔ You can lock the orientation if the rotating screen bothers you. See the section "Making Quick Settings," later in this chapter.

  ✔ This book shows the Home screen, as well as most other apps, in a horizontal orientation. See the later section, "Behold the Home Screen," for more information on the Home screen.

Controlling the volume

There are times when the sound level is too loud. There are times when it's too soft. And, there are those rare times when it's just right. Finding that just-right level is the job of the volume control buttons that cling to the left side of the Galaxy Tab.

Pressing the top part of the Volume button makes the volume louder; pressing the bottom part makes the volume softer. As you press the button, a graphic appears on the touchscreen to illustrate the relative volume level, as shown in Figure 3-1.

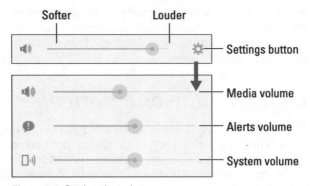

Figure 3-1: Setting the volume.

Touch the Settings button, shown in Figure 3-1, to see more detailed volume controls. You can individually set the volume for media, alerts, and the system, as shown in the expanded onscreen volume control: Drag the blue dot left or right to set the volume.

- Silencing the Tab by sliding down the volume level places it into Vibration mode.

- The Volume button works even when the Tab is locked (when the touchscreen display is off). That means you don't need to unlock the Tab if you're playing music and need to adjust the volume.

Behold the Home Screen

The main base from which you begin exploration of the Galaxy Tab is the *Home* screen. It's the first thing you see after unlocking the Tab, and the place you go to whenever you quit an application.

Touring the Home screen

The main Home screen for the Galaxy Tab is illustrated in Figure 3-2.

Figure 3-2: The Home screen.

There are several fun and interesting things to notice on the Home screen:

Google Search: Use this item to invoke a powerful search of the items stored on the Galaxy Tab or of the entire Internet.

Apps Menu button: Touch this button to view the collection of apps and widgets available on your tablet.

Home screen buttons: Special symbols are in the lower-left corner of the Home screen. The symbols identify buttons you touch to activate common Galaxy Tab features.

Notification icons: These icons come and go, depending on what happens in your digital life. For example, new icons appear whenever you receive a new e-mail message or have a pending appointment. The section "Reviewing notifications," later in this chapter, describes how to deal with notifications.

Status icons: These icons represent the Tab's current condition, such as the type of network it's connected to, signal strength, and battery status, as well as whether the Tab is connected to a Wi-Fi network or using Bluetooth, for example.

App icons: The meat of the meal on the Home screen plate is where the action takes place: app (application) icons. Touching an icon runs its program.

Widgets: A *widget* is a teensy program that can display information, let you control the Tab, access features, or do something purely amusing.

Ensure that you recognize the names of the various parts of the Home screen, because the terms are used throughout this book and in whatever other scant Galaxy Tab documentation exists. Directions for using the Home screen gizmos are found throughout this chapter.

Accessing multiple Home screens

The Home screen is more than what you see. It's actually an entire street of Home screens, with only one Home screen *page* displayed at a time.

To switch from one page to another, swipe the Home screen left or right. There are two pages to the left of the main Home screen page, and two pages to the right.

 When you touch the Home icon button, you're returned to the last Home screen page you viewed. To return to the main Home screen page, touch the Home icon button a second time.

Using the icon buttons

Festooning the Galaxy Tab Home screen are various symbols or icons. Those icons identify buttons you can touch. The icon buttons are used to control the Tab, seeing how the device lacks the necessary physical buttons. Table 3-1 lists the most common icon buttons.

Table 3-1	Common Icon Buttons	
Button	*Name*	*Function*
	Search	Search the Galaxy Tab or the Internet for some tidbit of information.
	Dictation	Use your voice to dictate text. On the Home screen dictation is used with the Google Search function.
	Apps Menu	Display the Apps Menu.
	Back	Go back, close, or dismiss the onscreen keyboard.
	Home	Go to the Home screen.
	Recent	Display recently opened apps.
	Screen Capture	Take a picture of the screen; see the section "Taking a screen cap."

The buttons listed in Table 3-1 are pretty common, available most of the time you use the Galaxy Tab. Beyond those buttons are other buttons and symbols used in the Tab's interface. They're listed in Table 3-2.

Table 3-2		Other Icon Buttons
Button	**Name**	**Function**
	Menu	This icon button displays the menu for an app. It's often found in the upper-right corner of the screen.
	Menu	Another icon for displaying a menu.
	Old Menu	This icon button is used primarily to display menus for older Android apps. It appears at the bottom of the screen, next to the Recent Apps icon button.
	Favorite	Touch the Favorite icon button to flag a favorite item, such as a contact or web page.
	Gear	The Gear icon button is used to display a settings menu or options for an app or feature.
	Settings	This Settings icon button is another version of the Gear icon button.
	Close	This button is used to close a window or clear text from an input field.
	Share	The Share icon button allows you to share information stored on the Tab via e-mail, social networking, or other Internet services.

Not every icon button always performs the actions listed in Table 3-2. For example, if there's no menu to open, pressing the Menu button does nothing.

> ✓ Various sections throughout this book give examples of using the icon buttons. Their images appear in the book's margins where relevant.

✔ The Google Search button may or may not have the word Google next to it. (Refer to Figure 3-2.) When the button is referenced in this book, only the magnifying glass is shown, as in Table 3-1.

✔ The Back icon button changes its appearance when the onscreen keyboard or recent apps list is displayed. It's still the Back icon button, but it changes appearance, as shown in the margin. Touch the button to dismiss the item that popped up on the screen.

✔ The little triangle in the lower-right corner of the Menu icon button is used in many apps to denote a pop-up or shortcut menu attached to something on the screen. Touch that triangle to see the shortcut menu.

✔ Other common symbols are used on icon buttons in various apps. For example, the standard Play/Pause icons are used as well as variations on the symbols shown in Tables 3-1 and 3-2.

Home Screen Chores

To become a cat, you must know how to perform several duties: Sleep, eat, catch critters, and cause mischief. A cat's life isn't difficult, and neither is your Galaxy Tab life, as long as you know how to do some basic duties on the Home screen. As with the cat, you have only a few duties to know about.

Starting an app

It's blissfully simple to run an app on the Home screen: Touch its icon. The app starts.

✔ Not all apps appear on the Home screen, but all of them appear when you display the Apps Menu screen. See the section "Visiting the Apps Menu," later in this chapter.

✔ When an app closes or you quit the application, you're returned to the Home screen.

✔ App is short for *application*.

Accessing a widget

Like app icons, widgets can appear on the Home screen. To use a widget, touch it. What happens next, of course, depends on the widget and what it does.

For example, touch the YouTube widget to view a video right on the Home screen; swipe your finger across that widget to peruse videos like you're flipping the pages in a book.

Other widgets do interesting things, display useful information, or give you access to the Galaxy Tab's features.

Reviewing notifications

Notifications appear as icons at the bottom right of the Home screen, as illustrated earlier, in Figure 3-2. To check out notifications, touch an icon or swipe up from the bottom-right onscreen. You see a scrolling list of all notifications, as shown in Figure 3-3.

Touch to act upon the notification   Close

Status info

Quick settings

Open Settings app

Notifications

Scroll down for more notifications   Dismiss all notifications

Figure 3-3: The Notification shade.

You can scroll through the list, as shown in Figure 3-3. To peruse a specific notification, touch it. To clear all the notifications, touch the Clear button.

 To hide the notification list, touch the Back icon button, the X (Close) button on the Notification shade (refer to Figure 3-3), or you can touch anywhere else on the Home screen.

- ✔ If you don't deal with the notifications, they can stack up!

- ✔ Notification icons disappear after they've been chosen.

- ✔ Dismissing some notifications doesn't prevent them from appearing again in the future. For example, notifications to update your programs continue to appear, as do calendar reminders.

- ✔ Some programs, such as Facebook and the various Twitter apps, don't display notifications unless you're logged in.

- ✔ The Galaxy Tab plays a sound, or *ringtone,* when a new notification floats in. You can choose which sound plays.

Making Quick Settings

The Quick Settings are a clutch of popular Tab features, each of which can be quickly accessed from the notifications pop-up (refer to Figure 3-3), though the full set of Quick Settings are shown in Figure 3-4. To see them all, you need to swipe the options left and right with your finger.

Figure 3-4: Galaxy Tab Quick Settings.

You can use several items in the Quick Settings list to manipulate various options on the Galaxy Tab:

Bluetooth: Turns the Tab's Bluetooth wireless radio on or off. See Chapter 10 for information on Bluetooth.

GPS: Turns on or off the Tab's global position system radio, which helps various apps pinpoint your location.

Sound: Places the Tab into silent-vibration mode. The Tab won't make a sound, but will instead vibrate when this option is set.

Airplane Mode: Disables the wireless radios not allowed while using the Tab on an airplane.

Screen Rotation: Enables the Tab's ability to rotate and reorient the touchscreen based on which way you're holding the Galaxy Tab. See the section "Changing the orientation," earlier in this chapter.

Power Saving: Activates the Tab's ability to save power when the battery is getting low.

Driving Mode: Sets options that make it easier to use the Tab while driving, such as dictation and text-to-speech options for reading e-mail.

Sync: Turns on background data synchronization with your Google account (and other Internet accounts).

In addition to the various buttons, the screen brightness slider is used to set how bright the touchscreen appears. Touch the Auto check box to enable automatic brightness based on ambient light. Otherwise, drag the dot left or right to make the screen brighter or darker, respectively (refer to Figure 3-3).

The last item in the Quick Settings area is titled Settings. It's not an on-off item, but rather a shortcut to the Settings app on the Apps Menu screen. You use the Settings app to control everything on the Galaxy Tab, not just the few Quick Settings items.

Popping up the mini-apps

A *mini-app* is a cross between an app and a widget. It generally does one specific thing or provides access to a handy tool. On your Galaxy Tab, the mini-apps dwell behind the bar across the bottom of the touchscreen. To display the mini-apps, touch the up-pointing chevron, illustrated in Figure 3-2.

There are a total of seven mini-apps, as shown in Figure 3-5, though your Galaxy Tab may have fewer mini-apps.

Mini-apps

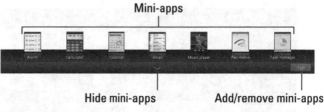

Hide mini-apps   Add/remove mini-apps

Figure 3-5: The mini-apps.

Start a mini-app by touching its icon. The mini-app appears centered on the touchscreen, floating above whatever other app you're using or the Home screen if you're at the Home screen.

Close the mini-app by touching the X button in the mini-app window's upper-right corner.

To hide the mini-apps, touch the down-pointing chevron, illustrated in Figure 3-5.

- Mini-apps are available any time you see the bar across the bottom of the screen.

- Use the Edit button (refer to Figure 3-5) to add or remove mini-apps. The collection of apps is limited to what appears on the Mini Apps menu.

- The Task Manager mini-app is used to view running apps. You can switch to a running app by touching its icon. You can also close any running app by touching the X button over the app's preview window.

Visiting the Apps Menu

The app icons you see on the Home screen don't represent all the apps in your Galaxy Tab. Those icons aren't even apps themselves; they're shortcuts. To see all apps installed on your Galaxy Tab, you must visit the Apps Menu screen. To do so, touch the Apps button on the Home screen. You see the Apps Menu, as shown in Figure 3-6.

View apps you've downloaded

Show apps   Show widgets   Menu button

Scroll to see more apps

Figure 3-6: The Apps Menu screen.

You can find any additional apps by swiping the Apps Menu screen to the left.

As you install apps, they're added to the Apps Menu. New apps are inserted into the Apps Menu alphabetically, which means that any time you add an app the Apps Menu gets re-sorted. That makes it difficult to locate apps by memory, though my advice is to place apps you use most often on the Home screen. You can also re-arrange the apps by touching the Menu button (refer to Figure 3-6) and choosing View Type⇨Customizable Grid.

To view only apps you've installed on your Galaxy Tab, touch Apps at the top of the Apps Menu screen, as shown in Figure 3-6.

✏ See Chapter 9 for information on getting more apps for your Galaxy Tab.

✏ The terms *program, application,* and *app* all mean the same thing.

Reviewing recent apps

 If you're like me, you probably use the same apps over and over on your Galaxy Tab. You can easily access that list of recent apps by touching the Recent Apps icon button on the Home screen. When you do, you see a pop-up list of apps most recently accessed.

 To reopen an app, choose it from the list. Otherwise, you can hide the recently used apps list by touching the Back (or Back-Hide) icon button.

Taking a screen cap

A screen cap (or capture) is a picture of your Galaxy Tab's touchscreen. To take the shot, touch the Screen Capture icon button, found at the bottom left of the Tab's screen (refer to Figure 3-2). You'll hear a click, maybe see some animation, and then whatever image was on the screen is saved as a picture file. Touch the Save button to save the image, or touch Cancel to discard it.

You can locate screen capture pictures in the Gallery app. They're found in the ScreenCapture album.

✔ There is no way to disable the Screen Capture icon button, at least not using the native tools supplied with your Galaxy Tab.

✔ Screen captures are standard .jpg graphics files. They're stored in the Pictures/Screenshots folder, found on the Tab's internal storage.

4
Typing and Text

*B*elieve it or not, the interface to the first computers had no monitor. Nope, computer scientists and proto-nerds of the 1960s used teletype machines. That was if they were lucky; before then punch cards were popular. But historically speaking, a physical keyboard has always been a part of the high tech scene. Until now.

Your Galaxy Tab lacks a real, live keyboard. All it has is a touchscreen, though you can use that touchscreen for typing. It works because of something called the *onscreen keyboard.* Not only that, but you can use your finger to edit and manipulate the text you type. Tab typing is a new concept. It can be frustrating. It can be strange. It can be understood and accepted if you follow my advice in this chapter.

The Old Hunt-and-Peck

The old mechanical typewriters required a lot of effort to press their keys. It was forceful: clackity-clack-clack. Electronic typewriters made typing easier. And, of course, the computer is the easiest thing to type on. A tablet? That device takes some getting used to because its keys are merely flat rectangles on a touchscreen. If this concept doesn't drive you nuts, typing on a tablet is something you should master with relative ease.

Using the onscreen keyboard

For text communications on the Galaxy Tab, you touch an onscreen keyboard. That keyboard pops up whenever the Tab requires text input or when you have an opportunity to type something.

The basic onscreen keyboard layout is shown in Figure 4-1. You'll be relieved to see that it's similar to the standard computer keyboard, though some of the keys change their function depending on what you're typing.

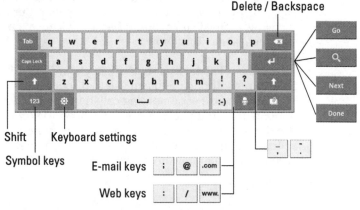

Figure 4-1: The onscreen keyboard.

Figure 4-1 illustrates the onscreen keyboard in Alphabetic mode. You see keys from A through Z in lowercase. You also see a Shift key for producing capital letters, and a Delete key, which works to backspace and erase.

The Enter key below the Delete key changes its look depending on what you're typing. Five variations are shown in Figure 4-1. Here's what each one does:

Enter/Return: Just like the Enter or Return key on your computer keyboard, this key ends a paragraph of text. It's used mostly when filling in long stretches of text or when multiline input is available.

Go: This action key directs the app to proceed with a search, accept input, or perform another action.

Search: You see the Search key appear when you're searching for something on the Tab. Touching the key starts the search.

Next: This key appears when you're typing information into multiple fields. Touching this key switches from one field to the next, such as when typing a username and password.

Done: This key appears whenever you've finished typing text in the final field of a screen that has several fields. Sometimes it dismisses the onscreen keyboard, sometimes not.

The large U key at the bottom center of the onscreen keyboard is the Space key. Next to it is the Smiley key, which inserts the colon, dash, and right parenthesis characters into your text, commonly known as the *smiley.*

Between the Space and Smiley keys, you'll occasionally see two sets of three additional keys. These sets of keys are used to assist when typing e-mail and web page addresses. The `.com` and `www.` keys insert all those characters with one key press.

The ! and ? keys also change, as shown in Figure 4-1: When typing in some situations, the exclamation point changes to an underline, and the question mark changes to a hyphen. When does that happen? I don't know, but watch out for it.

Also see the next section for accessing the number-and-symbol keys on the onscreen keyboard.

✔ To dismiss the onscreen keyboard, touch the Back-Hide icon button that replaces the standard Back icon button on the touchscreen.

✔ To re-summon the keyboard, touch any text field or spot on the screen where typing is permitted.

✔ Touch the Keyboard Settings (Gear) key to make adjustments to the onscreen keyboard.

✔ The keyboard reorients itself when you turn the Tab to a vertical position, though it's narrower and it may not be as easy on your fingers for typing.

✔ Some folks feel that the onscreen keyboard isn't complete unless there is a dictation button. See the section "Activating voice input on the keyboard," later in this chapter, for the secret instructions.

Accessing other symbols

You're not limited to typing only the symbols you see on the alphabetic keyboard, shown in Figure 4-1. The onscreen keyboard has many more symbols available, which you can see by touching the 123 key. Touching this key gives you access to three additional keyboard layouts, as shown in Figure 4-2.

Touch the 1/3, 2/3, or 3/3 key to switch between various symbol keyboards, as illustrated in Figure 4-2.

To return to the standard "alpha" keyboard (refer to Figure 4-1), touch the ABC key.

You can access special character keys from the main alphabetic keyboard, providing you know a secret: Long-press (touch and hold) a key. When you do, you see a pop-up palette of additional characters, similar to the ones shown for the A key in Figure 4-3.

Switch to
alpha keyboard   Switch to symbol keyboards

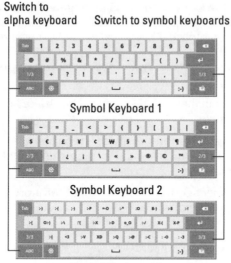

Symbol Keyboard 1

Symbol Keyboard 2

Symbol Keyboard 3

Figure 4-2: Number and symbol keyboards.

Figure 4-3: Special symbol pop-up palette thing.

Choose a character from the pop-up palette or touch the X button to close the pop-up palette.

Not every character has a special pop-up palette.

Typing duties

It's cinchy to type on the onscreen keyboard: Just press a letter to produce the character. It works just like a computer keyboard in that respect. Plus the keyboard is large enough in the Tab's horizontal orientation that you can almost touch-type.

As you type, the key you touch is highlighted. The Tab may give a wee bit of tactile feedback. It's easy to get used to, but I still find using a physical keyboard is the best way to type.

✔ Above all, it helps to *type slowly* until you get used to the keyboard.

✔ When you make a mistake, press the Delete key to back up and erase.

✔ A blinking cursor on the touchscreen shows where new text appears, which is similar to how text input works on your computer.

✔ See the later section, "Text Editing," for more details on editing your text.

Using predictive text

The Galaxy Tab is pretty smart when it comes to guessing the next word you're about to type. It's a feature called predictive text, and it can really speed up your input. Ensure that this feature is activated; obey these steps:

1. **Touch the Gear key (settings button) on the onscreen keyboard.**

2. **Choose XT9 Advanced Settings.**

3. **Place a check mark by the option Word Completion.**

4. **Touch the Back button twice to return to the app you were using where the onscreen keyboard was displayed.**

Once activated, the onscreen keyboard displays word suggestions as you type, similar to what's shown in Figure 4-4. Choose a word from the list by touching it with your finger, or by pressing the space key.

If you find the XT9 setting annoying (and many do), repeat the steps in this section to disable it.

Suggestions

Text you're typing   Show more suggestions

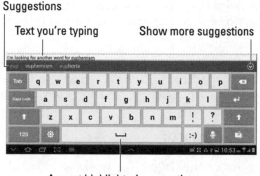

Accept highlighted suggestion

Figure 4-4: Automatic word selection.

Text Editing

You'll probably do more text editing on your Galaxy Tab than you realize. That includes the basic stuff, such as spiffing up typos and adding a period here or there as well as complex editing involving cut, copy, and paste. The concepts are the same as you find on a computer, but without a keyboard and mouse, the process can be daunting. This section irons out the text-editing wrinkles.

Moving the cursor

The first part of editing text is to move the cursor to the right spot. The *cursor* is that blinking, vertical line where text appears. On most computing devices, you move the cursor by using a pointing device. The Galaxy Tab has no pointing device, but you do: your finger.

To move the cursor, simply touch the spot on the text where you want to move the cursor. To help your precision, a cursor tab appears below the text, as shown in the margin. You can move that tab with your finger to move the cursor around in the text.

After you move the cursor, you can continue to type, use the Delete key to back up and erase, or paste in text copied from elsewhere.

You may see a pop-up by the cursor tab with a Paste command button in it. That button is used to paste in text, as described in the later section, "Cutting, copying, and pasting."

Selecting text

Selecting text on the Galaxy Tab works just like selecting text in a word processor: You mark the start and end of a block. That chunk of text appears highlighted on the screen.

Text-selection starts by long-pressing a chunk of text. Sometimes you have to press for a while, and you might try double-tapping the text, but eventually you see the Text Selection toolbar appear on the top of the screen. You also see a chunk of text selected, as shown in Figure 4-5.

Close the Text Selection toolbar   Text selection commands

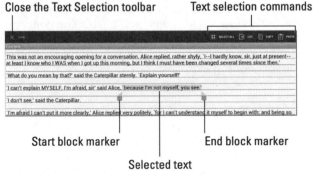

Start block marker   End block marker

Selected text

Figure 4-5: Tab text selection.

Drag the start and end markers around the touchscreen to define the block of selected text. Or you can touch the Select All command at the top of the screen to mark all the text as a single block. (Refer to Figure 4-5.)

After you select the text, you can delete it by touching the Delete key on the keyboard. You can replace the text by typing something new. Or you can cut or copy the text. See the section "Cutting, copying, and pasting," later in this chapter.

To cancel text selection, touch the Done button, or just touch anywhere on the touchscreen outside of the selected block.

✔ Seeing the onscreen keyboard is a good indication that you can edit and select text.

✔ Sometimes you may see a pop-up menu when you long-press text. If so, choose the Select Text command. You'll then see the Text Selection toolbar and be able to select text on the screen.

Selecting text on a web page

It's possible to select text from a web page even though the text there isn't "editable" text. Because the text isn't editable, or even edible, you need to follow these steps:

1. **Long-press the web page near the text you want to copy.**

   The start and end block markers appear, as does the Text Selection toolbar, though it doesn't look exactly like Figure 4-5: In addition to the Copy and Select All commands, there are Share, Find, and Web Search commands.

2. **Move the cursor tabs to mark the beginning and end of the block.**

3. **Choose Copy from the Text Selection toolbar.**

The text is copied into the Galaxy Tab clipboard. From there, it can be pasted into any app that accepts text input. See the next section.

✔ Copying text from a web page allows you to paste that text into an e-mail message or Facebook status update or into any field where you can paste text on the Galaxy Tab.

✔ The two other commands on the text-selection pop-up menu are Search and Share. Choose Search to look for text within the selected block. Choose the Share command to share the block as text or as an image via e-mail, instant message, Facebook, or any other sharing app installed on your Tab.

✔ Refer to Chapter 7 for more information on surfing the web with your Galaxy Tab.

Cutting, copying, and pasting

Selected text is primed for cutting or copying, which works just like it does in your favorite word processor. After you select the text, choose the proper command from the Text Selection toolbar: To copy the text, choose the Copy command. To cut the text, choose Cut.

Just like on your computer, cut or copied text on the Galaxy Tab is stored in a clipboard. To paste any previously cut or copied text, move the cursor to the spot where you want the text pasted.

If you're lucky, you'll see a Paste command button appear above the blinking cursor, as shown in Figure 4-6. If not, touch the cursor tab to see the Paste command button. Touch that command to paste in the text.

Figure 4-6: The Paste command button.

The Paste command can also be accessed from the Text Selection toolbar, although in that case the pasted text replaces any highlighted text on the screen.

The Paste command can be anywhere text is input on the Tab, such as in an e-mail message, a Twitter tweet, or any text field. Then touch the Paste icon that appears, as shown in Figure 4-6.

You can paste text only into locations where text is allowed. Odds are good that if you can type, or whenever you see the onscreen keyboard, you can paste text.

Galaxy Tab Dictation

The Galaxy Tab has the amazing ability to interpret your dictation as text. It works almost as well as computer dictation in science fiction movies, though I can't seem to find the command to launch photon torpedoes.

Activating voice input on the keyboard

To use dictation instead of typing, you need to activate voice input for the Samsung keypad. Obey these steps:

1. **Display the onscreen keyboard.**

   Touch a text box or somehow get the onscreen keyboard to appear.

2. **Touch the Settings button, the one with the Gear icon.**

3. **Touch the check box by Voice Input to place a green check mark there.**

4. **Touch the Yes button to confirm.**

   You can touch the Home icon button to return to the Home screen when you're done.

A new button now appears on the onscreen keyboard, near the bottom right. It's the Microphone button, as shown in the margin. Touch that button to dictate text instead of typing it.

Using voice input

Talking to your Tab really works, and works quite well, providing that you touch the Microphone key on the keyboard and properly dictate your text.

After touching the Microphone key, you see a special window appear on the bottom of the screen. When the text Speak Now appears, dictate your text; speak directly at the Tab.

As you speak, a Microphone graphic on the screen flashes. The flashing doesn't mean that the Galaxy Tab is embarrassed by what you're saying. No, the flashing merely indicates that the Tab is listening, detecting the volume of your voice.

After you stop talking, the Tab digests what you said. You see your voice input appear as a wavelike pattern on the screen. Eventually, the text you spoke — or a close approximation — appears on the screen. It's magical and sometimes comical.

✔ The first time you try voice input, you might see a description displayed. Touch the OK button to continue.

✔ The better your diction, the better your results. Also, it helps to speak only a sentence or less.

✔ You can edit your voice input just as you edit any text. See the section "Text Editing," earlier in this chapter.

✔ Speak the punctuation in your text. For example, you would say, "I'm sorry comma and it won't happen again" to have the Galaxy Tab produce the text I'm sorry, and it won't happen again (or similar wording).

✔ Common punctuation you can dictate includes the comma, period, exclamation point, question mark, and colon.

✔ Pause your speech before and after speaking punctuation.

- There is no way presently to capitalize words you dictate.

- Dictation may not work where no Internet connection exists.

5

All Your Friends in the Galaxy

In This Chapter

▶ Exploring the Contacts app
▶ Searching and sorting your contacts
▶ Adding new contacts
▶ Editing and changing contacts
▶ Deleting contacts

*A*s a communications device, your Galaxy Tab has a need to harbor information about all the people you know — specifically, those with whom you want to communicate electronically. From sending e-mail to social networking, you want to have access to your list of friends, pals, and cohorts. This chapter explains how do that on your Galaxy Tab.

Meet the Contacts App

You may already have some friends in your Galaxy Tab. That's because your Google account was synchronized with the Tab when you first set things up. Because all your Gmail and other types of contacts on the Internet were duplicated on the Tab, you already have a host of friends available. The place where you can access those folks is the Contacts app.

Using the Contacts app

To peruse the Galaxy Tab address book, start the Contacts app: Touch the Apps Menu icon button on the Home screen; then touch the Contacts app icon.

The Contacts app shows a list of all contacts in your Galaxy Tab, organized alphabetically by first name, similar to the ones shown in Figure 5-1.

Add a new contact

Quickly scroll   Contact name   Edit contact

Search contacts

Contact groups   Contact picture   Favorite button   Delete contact

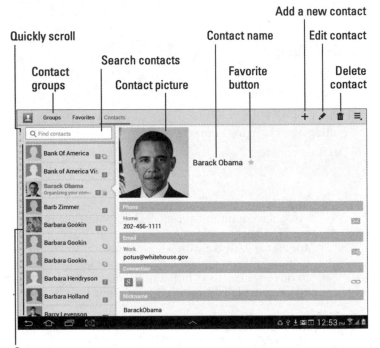

Contacts

Figure 5-1: Your Galaxy Tab address book.

Scroll the list by swiping with your finger. Or, you can drag your finger on the left side of the screen to quickly scan through the list, as shown in Figure 5-1.

To do anything with a contact, you first have to choose it: Touch a contact name, and you see detailed information in the right side of the screen, as shown in Figure 5-1. The list of activities you can do with the contact depends on the information shown and the apps installed on the tab. Here are some options:

Place a phone call: Yes, the Tab is not a phone, but when you install Skype, touching a contact's phone number activates that app, and you can use the Tab to make a call.

Send e-mail: Touch the contact's e-mail address to compose an e-mail message using either the Gmail or Email app. When the contact has more than one e-mail address, you can choose to which one you want to send the message. Chapter 6 covers using e-mail on your Tab.

View address: When the contact has a home or business address, you can choose that item to view the address using the Maps app. You can then get directions, look at the place using the Street View tool, or do any of a number of interesting things.

View social networking status: Contacts who are also your social networking buddies show their current status. The status might also appear at the bottom of the info list, there may be a View Profile item to choose, or you may see a Social Network Feeds button, which lets you see all of the contact's social networking status updates.

Sorting your contacts

Your contacts are displayed in the Contacts app in a certain order: alphabetically by first name, first name first. You can change that order if you like. Here's how:

1. **Start the Contacts app.**

2. **Touch the Menu icon button.**

3. **Choose Settings.**

   The Settings screen appears, which shows you the settings for viewing your contacts.

4. **Choose the List By command to specify how contacts are sorted: by First Name or Last Name.**

   The Contacts app is configured to show contacts by First Name.

5. **Choose Display Contacts By to specify how the contacts appear in the list: First Name First or Last Name First.**

   The Contacts app shows the contacts listed by First Name First.

There's no right or wrong way to display your contacts — only whichever method you're used to. I prefer them sorted by last name and listed first name first.

Searching contacts

You can have a massive number of contacts. Though the Contacts app doesn't provide a running total, I'm certain that I have more than 500 contacts on my Tab. That number combines my Facebook, Gmail, Twitter, and other accounts. I have a lot of contacts, and I have the potential for even more contacts.

Rather than endlessly scroll the Contacts list and run the risk of rubbing your fingers to nubs, you can employ the Galaxy Tab's powerful Search command. Type the name you want to locate in the Find Contacts text box at the top of the screen, as shown in Figure 5-1. The list of contacts quickly narrows to show only the contacts that contain the text you type.

To clear a search, touch the X button, found at the right side of the Find Contacts text box.

All Your Friends in the Galaxy Tab

There are two primary things you can do with the Contacts app besides looking up the people you know. The first thing, and possibly the most rewarding thing personally, is to add more contacts. The second thing, which is necessary when the first thing becomes wildly successful, is organizing those people. This section covers both duties.

Adding contacts

There are more ways to put contacts into your Galaxy Tab than you're probably aware of. This section lists a few of the more popular and useful methods.

Create a new contact from scratch

Sometimes it's necessary to create a contact when you actually meet another human being in the real world, or maybe you finally got around to transferring information into the Tab from your old, paper address book. In either instance, you have information to input, and it starts like this:

1. **Open the Contacts app.**

2. **Touch the Add Contact button (refer to Figure 5-1).**

3. **Choose your Google account from the menu.**

   I recommend creating new contacts using Google because it synchronizes the information with the Internet and any other Android gizmos you may own.

4. **Fill in the information on the New Contact screen (shown in Figure 5-2) as best you can.**

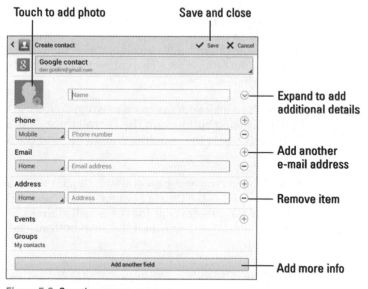

Figure 5-2: Creating a new contact.

Use the chevron (down-arrow) button to expand an area to see more details. To add fields, touch the Plus button; touch the Minus button to remove a field.

5. **Touch the Done button to complete editing and add the new contact.**

The new contact is automatically synched with your Google account. That's one beauty of the Android operating system used by the Galaxy Tab: You have no need to duplicate your efforts; contacts you create on the Tab are instantly updated with your Google account on the Internet.

✔ Use the Add Another Field button when you don't see enough fields to add information required for a contact.

✔ Touching the triangle buttons (refer to Figure 5-2) displays pop-up menus from which you can choose various options, such as setting whether a phone number or an e-mail address is Home, Business, or what have you.

✔ Information from social networking sites is stirred into the Contacts list automatically, though sometimes the process creates duplicate entries. See the section "Joining identical contacts" for how to remedy such a situation.

Create a contact from an e-mail message

Perhaps one of the easiest ways to build up the contacts list is to create a new contact from an e-mail message. It's simple: When reading the e-mail message, touch the contact's name button in the From field. (The contact's name is a button.) A pop-up window appears.

To add the e-mail address to an existing contact, touch the Update Existing button, and then scroll through the list of contacts. Choose the matching contact to add the new e-mail address.

To add the person as a new contact, touch the Create Contact button. You'll see the Create Contact screen (refer to Figure 5-2). Fill in the blanks — except for the e-mail address, which is already filled-in — then touch the Save button. The contact is created.

Importing contacts from your computer

Your computer's e-mail program is doubtless a useful repository of contacts you've built up over the years. You can export these contacts from your computer's e-mail program and then import them into the Galaxy Tab. It's not easy, but it's possible.

The key is to save or export your computer e-mail program's records in the *vCard* (.vcf) file format. These records can then be imported by the Galaxy Tab into the Contacts app. The method for exporting contacts varies depending on the e-mail program:

- ✔ **In the Windows Live Mail program,** choose Go⟡ Contacts and then choose File⟡Export⟡Business Card (.VCF) to export the contacts.

- ✔ **In Windows Mail,** choose File⟡Export⟡Windows Contacts and then choose vCards (Folder of .VCF Files) from the Export Windows Contacts dialog box. Click the Export button.

- ✔ **On the Mac,** open the Address Book program and choose File⟡Export⟡Export vCard.

After the vCard files are created on your computer, connect the Galaxy Tab to the computer and transfer them. Transferring files from your computer to the Galaxy Tab is covered in Chapter 11.

After the vCard files have been copied to the Tab, follow these steps in the Contacts app to complete the process:

1. **Touch the Menu icon button.**

2. **Choose the Import/Export command.**

3. **Choose Import from USB Storage.**

4. **Choose your Google account.**

5. **Choose the option Import All vCard Files**

6. **Touch the OK button.**

   The contacts are saved on your Tab but will also be synchronized to your Gmail account, which instantly creates a backup copy.

The importing process may create some duplicates. That's okay: You can join two entries for the same person in the Contacts app. See the section "Joining identical contacts," later in this chapter.

Grab contacts from your social networking sites

You can pour your whole gang of friends and followers into the Galaxy Tab from your social networking sites. The operation is automatic: Simply add the social networking site to the Tab's inventory of apps. The social networking contacts are instantly added to the Contacts app list. (See Chapter 9 for more on apps.)

Find a new contact on the map

When you use the Maps app to locate a coffee house, apothecary, or parole office (or all three in one place), you can quickly create a contact for that location. Here's how:

1. **After searching for your location, touch the cartoon bubble that appears on the map.**

   You see more details for the location on the left side of the screen.

2. **Touch the Menu icon button in the upper-right corner of the screen.**

3. **Choose Add As a Contact.**

   You see the New Contact screen with much of the information already filled in. That's because the Maps app shared that info with the Contacts app.

4. **Optionally, add more information if you know it.**

5. **Touch the Save button.**

   The new contact is created.

Editing a contact

To make minor touch-ups on any contact, start by locating and displaying the contact's information. Touch the Edit icon button (refer to Figure 5-1), and start making changes.

Change or add information by touching a field and typing on the onscreen keyboard. You can edit information as well: Touch the field to edit and change whatever you want.

Some information cannot be edited. For example, fields pulled in from social networking sites can be edited only by that account holder on the social networking site.

When you're finished editing, touch the Save button.

Add an image for a contact

The simplest way to add a picture to one of your Galaxy Tab contacts is to have the image already stored in the Tab. You can snap a picture and save it, grab a picture from the Internet (covered in Chapter 7), or use any image already stored in the Tab's Gallery app. The image doesn't even have to be a picture of the contact — any image will do.

After the contact's photo, or any other suitable image, is stored on the Tab, follow these steps to update the contact's information:

1. **Locate and display the contact's information.**

2. **Touch the Edit icon button, which looks like a pencil.**

3. **Touch the Contact Picture icon (refer to Figure 5-1).**

4. **Choose Picture.**

   If you have other image management apps on your Tab, you can choose the app's command from the list. Otherwise:

5. **Choose Gallery.**

   The photo gallery is displayed. It lists all photos and videos stored on your Galaxy Tab.

6. **Browse the photo gallery to look for a suitable image.**

7. **Touch the image you want to use for the contact.**

8. **Crop the image.**

   Use Figure 5-3 as a guide for how to crop the image.

Crop image

Drag cropping box   Resize cropping box | Cancel

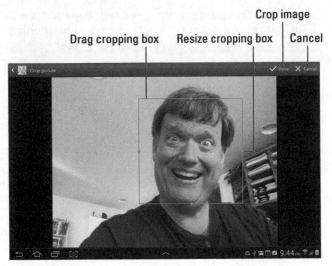

Figure 5-3: Cropping a contact's image.

9. **Touch the Done button.**

   The image is cropped but not yet assigned:

10. **Touch the Save button to finish editing the contact.**

   The image is now assigned, and it appears whenever the contact is referenced on your Galaxy Tab.

You can add pictures to contacts on your Google account by using any computer. Just visit your Gmail Contacts list to edit a contact. You can then add to that contact any picture stored on your computer. The picture is eventually synced with the same contact on your Galaxy Tab.

Make a favorite

A *favorite* contact is someone you stay in touch with most often. The person doesn't have to be someone you like — just someone you (perhaps unfortunately) contact often, such as your bookie.

The favorite contacts are kept in the Favorites group, which can be chosen from the top of the Contact's app screen. (Refer to Figure 5-1.) There are also other apps and widgets that make use of your favorite contacts.

To add a contact to the Favorites group, display the contact's information and touch the Star button by the contact's image. When the star is orange, the contact is marked as one of your favorites.

To remove a favorite, touch the contact's star again, and it loses its color. Removing a favorite doesn't delete the contact but instead removes it from the Favorites group.

Manage Your Friends

Nothing is truly perfect the first time, especially when you create things on a Galaxy Tab while typing with your thumbs at 34,000 feet during turbulence. You can do a whole slate of things with your Galaxy Tab contacts. This section covers the more interesting and useful things.

Joining identical contacts

Because the Galaxy Tab can pull contacts from multiple sources (Facebook, Gmail, Twitter), you may discover duplicate contact entries in the Contacts app. Rather than fuss over which entry to use, you can join the contacts. Here's how:

1. **Wildly scroll the Contacts list until you locate a duplicate.**

   Well, maybe not *wildly* scroll, but locate a duplicated entry. Because the Contacts list is sorted, the duplicates appear close together (though that may not always be the case).

2. **Select one of the contacts to view it on the right side of the screen.**

 3. **Touch the Menu icon button.**

4. **Choose Join Contact.**

   The Join Contact(s) window appears, listing your contacts.

5. **Choose a contact to join, the same person but from a different source.**

   The accounts are merged. Well, they appear together on your Galaxy Tab.

Removing a contact

Every so often, consider reviewing your contacts. Purge those folks whom you no longer recognize or you've forgotten. It's simple: Touch the Trash icon found at the top of the screen when you're viewing a contact. Touch the OK button to confirm. The contact is gone.

Because the Contacts list is synchronized with your Gmail contacts for your Google account, the contact is also removed there.

For some linked accounts, such as Facebook, deleting the account from your Tab doesn't remove the human from your Facebook account. In fact, some linked social networking accounts cannot be removed. The Tab rudely reminds you of that fact should you try.

6

Mail of the Electronic Kind

I'll bet it's been a long time since you've asked someone for his e-mail address and he didn't have one. Probably longer still since someone responded, "E-mail? What's that?" It would probably be odder still if people asked why there's a dash in "e-mail" now, when in my books published before 2010 there wasn't, but I'm getting sidetracked.

To help keep you electronically connected, the Galaxy Tab features the ability to collect and send your electronic missives. You can read and compose just about anywhere you go, peruse attachments, forward messages, and do the entire e-mail e-nchilada all in one spot.

Galactic E-Mail

Electronic mail is handled on the Galaxy Tab by two apps: Gmail and Email.

The Gmail app hooks directly into your Google Gmail account. In fact, they're exact echoes of each other: The Gmail you receive on your computer is also received on your Tab.

You can also use the Email app to connect with non-Gmail electronic mail, such as the standard mail service provided by your ISP or a web-based e-mail system such as Yahoo! Mail or Windows Live Mail.

Regardless of the app, electronic mail on the Galaxy Tab works just like it does on your computer: You can receive mail, create new messages, forward e-mail, send messages to a group of contacts, and work with attachments, for example. As long as there's a data connection, e-mail works just peachy.

- ✔ Both the Gmail and Email apps are located on the Apps Menu.

- ✔ The Email app can be configured to handle multiple e-mail accounts, as discussed later in this section.

- ✔ Although you can use your Tab's web browser to visit the Gmail website, you should use the Gmail app to pick up your Gmail.

Setting up an Email account

The Email app is used to access web-based e-mail, or *webmail,* such as Yahoo!, Windows Live, and others. It also lets you read e-mail provided by your Internet service provider (ISP), office, or other large, intimidating organization. To get things set up regardless of the service, follow these steps:

1. Start the Email app.

Look for it on the Apps Menu, along with all other apps on your Tab.

If you haven't yet run the Email app, the first screen you see is Account Setup. Continue with Step 2. Otherwise you're taken to the Email inbox: See the next section for information on adding additional e-mail accounts.

2. **Type the e-mail address you use for the account.**

3. **Type the password for that account.**

4. **Touch the Next button.**

   If you're lucky, everything is connected smoothly. Otherwise you'll have to specify the details as provided by your ISP. That includes the incoming and outgoing server information, often known by the bewildering acronyms POP3 and SMTP. Plod through the steps on the screen, though you'll primarily need to specify only the incoming and outgoing server names.

   Eventually you'll end up at the Account Options screen.

5. **Set the account options on the aptly named Account Options screen.**

   You might want to reset the Inbox Checking Frequency to something other than 15 minutes.

   If the account is to be your main e-mail account, place a green check mark by the option Send Email from This Account by Default.

6. **Touch the Next button.**

7. **Give the account a name and check your own name.**

   The account is given the name of the mail server, which may not ring a bell with you when it comes to receiving your e-mail. I name my ISP's e-mail account Main because it's my main account.

   The Your Name field lists your name as it's applied to outgoing messages. So if your name is really Wilma Flagstone and not `wflag4457`, you can make that change now.

8. **Touch the Next button.**

   You're done.

The next thing you'll see will be your e-mail account inbox. See the section "You've Got E-Mail" for what to do next.

Adding even more e-mail accounts

The Email app can be configured to pick up mail from multiple sources. If you have a Yahoo! Mail or Windows Live account, or maybe your corporate account, in addition to your ISP's account, you can add them. Follow through with these steps:

1. **Visit the Apps Menu and start the Settings app.**

2. **Choose Accounts & Sync.**

3. **Touch the Add Account button.**

4. **If your account type is shown in the list, such as Yahoo! Mail, choose it. Otherwise, choose the Email icon.**

5. **Type the account's e-mail address.**

6. **Type the password for the account.**

7. **Touch the Next button.**

   In a few magical moments, the e-mail account is configured and added to the account list.

   If you goofed up the account name or password, you're warned: Try again. Or if the account requires additional setup, use the information provided by the ISP or other source to help you fill in the appropriate fields.

8. **Set account options.**

   Most of the preset choices are fine for a web-based e-mail account.

   If the account is your primary e-mail account, place a green check mark by the option Send Email from This Account by Default.

   You might also consider a more frequent update interval, especially if you get a lot of mail or need to respond to it quickly.

9. **Touch the Next button.**

10. **Name the account and confirm your name.**

Feel free to change both the account name and your own name.

11. **Touch the Next button.**

The account is added to the list on the My Accounts screen.

You can repeat the steps in this section to add more e-mail accounts. All the accounts you configure will be made available through the Email app.

You've Got E-Mail

The Galaxy Tab works flawlessly with Gmail. In fact, if Gmail is already set up to be your main e-mail address, you'll enjoy having access to your messages all the time by using your Tab.

Non-Gmail e-mail, handled by the Email app, must be set up before it can be used, as covered earlier in this chapter. After completing the quick and occasionally painless setup, you can receive e-mail on your Tab just as you can on a computer.

Getting a new message

You're alerted to the arrival of a new e-mail message in your Tab by a notification icon. The icon differs depending on the e-mail's source.

 For a new Gmail message, you see the New Gmail notification (shown in the margin) appear at the top of the touchscreen.

 For a new e-mail message, you see the New Email notification.

Touch the notification icon at the bottom of the screen to see a summary of the most recent message. When multiple messages are waiting, you'll see a number indicating how many. Touching the notification's pop-up window takes you to either the Gmail or Email app where you can read the message.

To deal with the new-message notification, drag down the notifications and choose the appropriate one. You're taken directly to your inbox to read the new message.

Checking the inbox

To peruse your Gmail, start the Gmail app. You can find it on the main Home screen or on the Apps Menu. The Gmail inbox is shown in Figure 6-1.

Figure 6-1: The Gmail inbox.

To check your Email inbox, open the Email app. You're taken to the inbox for your primary e-mail account.

When you have multiple e-mail accounts accessed through the Email app, you can view your universal inbox by choosing the Combined View command from the Account menu, as shown in Figure 6-2.

New message

Mailbox overview   Refresh | Forward

Account menu   Search | Reply

Click to select message   Delete message

Figure 6-2: Messages in the Email app.

Notice that your Gmail inbox is missing from the Combined View window. (Refer to Figure 6-2.) Gmail is its own app; your Gmail messages don't show up in the universal inbox.

✒ Search your Gmail messages by pressing the Search button, as shown in Figure 6-1.

✒ Gmail is organized using labels, not folders. To see your Gmail labels from the inbox, touch the Folder Overview button. It's found in the upper-left corner of the screen.

✒ The Email app is used to access your primary non-Gmail e-mail account. The Messaging app is used to access all non-Gmail accounts.

✒ Scroll the message list in the Email app to view older messages. The Newer and Older buttons move you through the messages one at a time.

Reading an e-mail message

As mail comes in, you can read it by choosing a new e-mail notification, as described earlier in this chapter. Reading and working with the message operate much the same whether you're using the Gmail or Email app.

Choose a message to read by touching the message on the left side of the screen, as illustrated in Figures 6-1 and 6-2. The message text appears on the right side of the window, which you can scroll up or down by using your finger.

To access additional e-mail commands, touch the Menu icon button. The commands available depend on what you're doing in the Gmail or Email app at the time you touch the button.

- Starred messages can be viewed or searched separately, making them easier to locate later.

- If you properly configure the Email program, there's no need to delete messages you read.

Write That Message

Every so often, someone comes up to me and says, "Dan, you're a computer freak. You probably get a lot of e-mail." I generally nod and smile. Then the person ponders, "How can I get more e-mail?" The answer is simple: To get mail, you have to send mail. Or, you can just be a jerk on a blog and leave your e-mail address there. That method works too, though I don't recommend it.

Composing a new message

Crafting an e-mail epistle on your Tab works exactly like creating one on your computer. Figure 6-3 shows the basic setup for the Gmail app; the Email app is similar.

Here's how to get there:

1. **Start an e-mail app, either Gmail or Email.**

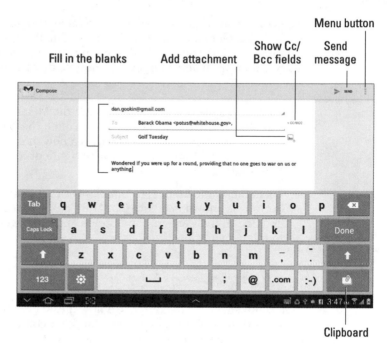

Menu button

Show Cc/   Send

Fill in the blanks   Add attachment   Bcc fields   message

Clipboard

Figure 6-3: Writing a new e-mail message.

2. **Touch the Compose icon button.**

3. **Touch the To field and type the e-mail address.**

You can type the first few letters of a contact name and then choose a matching contact from the list that's displayed.

4. **Type a subject.**

5. **Type the message.**

6. **Touch the Send button to whisk your missive to the Internet for immediate delivery.**

To send the message later, save it as a draft: In the Gmail app, touch the Menu button and choose Save Draft. In the Email app, touch the Save icon (which looks like an old floppy disk). The message is stored in the Drafts folder. You can open this folder to edit the message. Touch Send to send it.

Copies of the messages you send in the Email program are stored in the Sent mailbox. If you're using Gmail, copies are saved in your Gmail account, which you can access from your Galaxy Tab or from any computer or mobile device connected to the Internet.

> ✔ To cancel a message in Gmail, touch the Menu button and choose the Discard command. Touch the OK button to confirm. In the Email app, cancel a new message by touching the X button in the upper-right corner of the New Mail window.

> ✔ To summon the Cc field in Gmail, press the +Cc/Bcc button, as shown in Figure 6-3. The Cc (Carbon Copy) and Bcc (Blind Carbon Copy) fields appear, eager for you to fill them in.

Sending e-mail to a contact

A quick and easy way to compose a new message is to find a contact and then create a message using that contact's information. Heed these steps:

1. **Open the Contacts app.**

   See Chapter 5 for details.

2. **Locate the contact to whom you want to send an electronic message.**

   Review Chapter 5 for ways to hunt down contacts in a long list.

3. **Touch the contact's e-mail address.**

4. **Choose the Compose command to send an e-mail message using the Email app; choose Gmail to send the message using Gmail.**

   Other options may appear on the complete Action Using menu. For example, a custom e-mail app you've downloaded may show up there as well.

At this point, creating the message works as described in the preceding section; refer there for additional information.

Message Attachments

Attachments on the Galaxy Tab work pretty much the same in both the Gmail and Email apps. The key is the paperclip icon, not only for receiving attachments, but for sending them as well.

Dealing with attachments

The Galaxy Tab lets you view or save most e-mail attachments, depending on what's attached. You can also send attachments, though it's more of a computer activity, not something that's completely useful on a mobile device; the Tab isn't really designed for creating or manipulating information.

Email messages with attachments are flagged in the inbox with the paperclip icon, which seems to be the standard I-have-an-attachment icon for most e-mail programs. When you open one of these messages, you may see the attachment right away, specifically if it's a picture.

When you don't see the attachment right away, you see buttons in the message, which you can touch to view or save the attachment.

 ✔ Touch the Preview button to witness the attachment on your Tab.

 ✔ Touch the View button to download and see the attachment.

 ✔ Touch the Save button to save the attachment without viewing it.

What happens after you touch the Preview or View button depends on the type of attachment. Sometimes you see a list of apps from which you can choose one to open the attachment. Many Microsoft Office documents are opened by the Quickoffice app.

Some attachments cannot be opened. In these cases, use a computer to fetch the message and attempt to open the attachment. Or, you can reply to the message and inform the sender that you cannot open the attachment on your Galaxy Tab.

Sometimes, pictures included in an e-mail message aren't displayed. You find the Show Pictures button in the message, which you can touch to display the pictures.

Sending an attachment

The most common thing to send from the Galaxy Tab as an e-mail attachment is a picture or video. You're not limited to only pictures, though. You can attach documents you've previously saved on the Tab, music, or even random files if you're so bold.

The key to adding an attachment to an outgoing message is to touch the paperclip icon in the Compose window. This technique works in both the Gmail and Email apps. After touching the Add Attachment icon, you see the Choose Attachment menu. The number of items on that menu depends on what's installed on your Galaxy Tab. There are a few basic items:

Gallery: Pluck a picture or video from the Tab's Gallery app.

Quickoffice: Choose a document that you've saved on your Galaxy Tab.

Select music track: Choose music saved on your Galaxy Tab.

Other items: If you've installed another photo manager or a file manager, it also appears on the list.

The number of items you see depends on what's installed on the Galaxy Tab. Also the variety is different between the Gmail and Email apps.

You'll use the program you've chosen to locate the specific file or media tidbit you plan on sending. That item is attached to the outgoing message.

To select more than one attachment, touch the paperclip icon again.

It's also possible to send an attachment by using the various Share commands and buttons located in apps throughout the Galaxy Tab. After choosing the Share command, select Gmail or Email as the app to use for sharing whatever it is you want to share.

7

Tablet Web Browsing

. . . .

In This Chapter

▶ Browsing the web on your Tab

▶ Adding a bookmark

▶ Working with tabs

▶ Saving web pages

▶ Downloading images and files

▶ Setting a new home page

▶ Configuring the Internet app

. . . .

*T*he World Wide Web was designed to be viewed on a computer. The monitor is big and roomy. Web pages are displayed amply, like Uncle Jeff on the sofa watching a ballgame. The smaller the screen, however, the more difficult it is to view web pages designed for those roomy monitors. The web on a cell phone? Tragic. But on the Galaxy Tab, the web just seems to fit.

The Galaxy Tab has a nice, roomy screen. Viewing the web on the Tab is like seeing a younger, thinner version of Uncle Jeff sitting in the Hepplewhite. It's enjoyable, especially when you've read the good information in this chapter on surfing the web with your Galaxy Tab.

If possible, activate the Galaxy Tab's Wi-Fi connection before you venture out on the web. Though you can use the Tab's cellular data connection, the Wi-Fi connection incurs no data usage charges.

Mobile Web Browsing

Rare is the person these days who has had no experience with the World Wide Web. More common is someone who has used the web on a computer but has yet to taste the Internet waters on a mobile device. If that's you, consider this section your quick mobile web orientation.

Viewing the web

Your Galaxy Tab's web-browsing app is named Internet. You may find its icon on the main Home screen or, like all the other apps on the Tab, it's on the Apps Menu. Figure 7-1 illustrates the Internet app's interface.

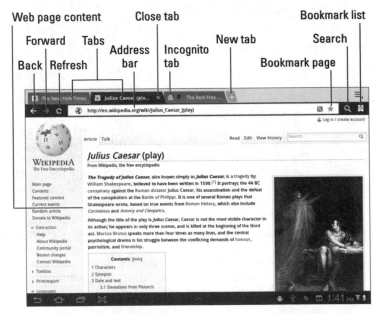

Figure 7-1: The Internet app.

Here are some handy Galaxy Tab web-browsing tips:

✔ Pan the web page by dragging your finger across the touchscreen. You can pan up, down, left, or right when the page is larger than the Tab's screen.

✔ Pinch the screen to zoom out or spread two fingers to zoom in.

✔ You can orient the Tab vertically to read a web page in Portrait mode. Doing so may reformat some web pages, which can make long lines of text easier to read.

Visiting a web page

To visit a web page, type its address into the Address box. (Refer to Figure 7-1.) You can also type a search word or phrase if you don't know the exact address of a web page. Touch the Go button on the onscreen keyboard to search the web or visit a specific web page.

If you don't see the Address box, touch the web page's tab atop the screen. The Address box, along with the various buttons left and right, appears on the screen.

You "click" links on a page by touching them with your finger. If you have trouble stabbing the right link, zoom in on the page and try again.

✔ When typing a web page address, use the www. key to instantly type those characters for the address. The www. key changes to the .com key to assist you in rapidly typing those characters as well.

✔ To reload a web page, touch the Refresh symbol on the left end of the Address bar.

✔ To stop a web page from loading, touch the X that appears to the left of the Address bar. The X replaces the Refresh button and appears only when a web page is loading.

Browsing back and forth

To return to a web page, you can touch the Browser's Back button, shown here and in Figure 7-1, or press the Back icon button at the bottom of the screen.

Touch the Browser's Forward button to go forward or to
return to a page you were visiting before you touched the
Back button.

To review the long-term history of your web-browsing adven-
tures, touch the Bookmarks button in the upper-right corner
of the Browser window, as shown in Figure 7-2. Choose the
History tab to view your web-browsing history.

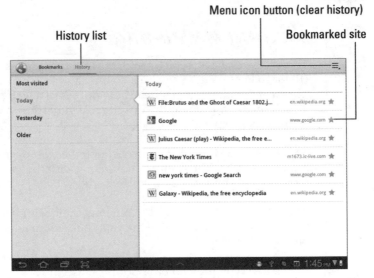

Figure 7-2: The Browser's history list.

To view a page you visited weeks or months ago, you can
choose a web page from the History list.

To clear the History list, touch the Menu icon button, shown
in Figure 7-2, and choose the Clear History command.

Using bookmarks

Bookmarks are those electronic breadcrumbs you can drop
as you wander the web. Need to revisit a website? Just look

up its bookmark. This advice assumes, of course, that you bother to create (I prefer *drop*) a bookmark when you first visit the site.

The cinchy way to bookmark a page is to touch the Favorite (star) icon on the right end of the Address bar. Tap that icon, and you see the Add Bookmark window, shown in Figure 7-3.

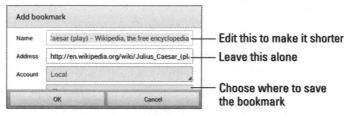

Figure 7-3: Adding a bookmark.

I edit the Label to something shorter, especially if the web page's title is long. Shorter names look better on the Bookmarks window. Touch the OK button and you've added the bookmark.

After the bookmark is set, it appears in the list of bookmarks. To see the list, touch the Bookmarks button on the Internet app's main window. (Refer to Figure 7-1.) You see a list of web page thumbnails with their labels or titles beneath. Swipe the list downward to see more bookmarks and thumbnails.

Touch a bookmark to visit that page.

✔ You can add a bookmark to the Home screen by long-pressing the bookmark thumbnail. Choose the Add Shortcut to Home command from the menu.

✔ Remove a bookmark by long-pressing its entry in the Bookmarks list. Choose the command Delete Bookmark. Touch the OK button to confirm. The bookmark is gone.

✔ The MyBookmarks app, available at the Google Play Store, can import your Internet Explorer, Firefox, and Chrome bookmarks from your Windows computer into the Galaxy Tab. See Chapter 9 for more information on the Google Play Store.

Managing web pages in multiple tabs

The Internet app uses a tabbed interface to display more than one web page at a time. Refer to Figure 7-1 to see various tabs marching across the Internet app's screen, just above the Address bar.

Here's how you work the tabbed interface:

✔ *To open a blank tab,* touch the plus button to the right of the last tab, as shown in Figure 7-1.

✔ *To open a link in a new tab,* long-press that link. Choose the command Open in New Window from the menu that appears. (The command should read Open in New Tab, and it may be changed in the future.)

✔ *To open a bookmark in a new window,* long-press the bookmark and choose the command Open in New Tab.

You switch between tabs by choosing one from the top of the screen.

Close a tab by touching its X (Close) button; you can close only the tab you're currently viewing.

For secure browsing, you can open an *incognito tab:* Press the Menu icon button and choose the command New Incognito Tab. When you go incognito, the Internet app won't track your history, leave cookies, or other evidence of which web pages you've visited in the incognito tab. A short description appears on the incognito tab page describing how it works.

Searching the web

The handiest way to find things on the web is to use the Google widget, shown in Figure 7-4. That widget appears in the upper-left corner of every Home screen page. Touch the widget to activate it.

Figure 7-4: The Google widget.

To search for something anytime you're viewing a web page in the Internet app, touch the Search icon button, found on the right end of the Address bar. Type the search term into the Address box. You can choose from a list of suggestions.

To find text on the web page you're looking at, as opposed to searching the entire Internet, follow these steps:

1. **Visit the web page where you want to find a specific tidbit o' text.**

2. **Press the Menu icon button.**

3. **Choose Find on Page.**

4. **Type the text you're searching for.**

5. **Use the left- or right-arrow button to locate that text on the page — backward or forward, respectively.**

   The found text appears highlighted in green.

6. **Touch the Done button when you're finished searching.**

Saving a web page

I like to save some web pages for later reading. It's not an obvious thing to do, but I save the web pages of long diatribes or interesting text so that I can read them later, such as when I'm cooped up in an airplane for a cross-country trip, sitting around bored at the car repair shop, or visiting other locations where time slows and boredom grows.

To save a web page, follow these steps:

1. **Visit the page you want to save.**

2. **Touch the Menu icon button and choose the command Save for Offline Reading.**

   The page is saved to the Tab's internal storage.

The web page is saved in the Saved Pages folder. You can view the page by touching the Bookmarks button and then choosing the Saved Pages tab from the top of the screen.

The Art of Downloading

There's nothing to downloading, other than understanding that most people use the term without knowing exactly what it means. Officially, a *download* is a transfer of information over a network from another source to your gizmo. For your Galaxy Tab, that network is the Internet, and the other source is a web page.

- ✔ The Downloading complete notification appears after the Galaxy Tab has downloaded something. You can choose that notification to view the download.

- ✔ There's no need to download program files to the Galaxy Tab. If you want new software, you can obtain it from the Google Play Store, covered in Chapter 9.

Grabbing an image from a web page

The simplest thing to download is an image from a web page. It's cinchy: Long-press the image. You see a pop-up menu appear, from which you choose the command Save Image.

To view images you download from the web, you use the Gallery app. Downloaded images are saved in the Download album.

Technically, the image is stored on the Tab's internal storage. It can be found in the `download` folder. You can read about Galaxy Tab file storage in Chapter 11.

Downloading a file

The web is full of links that don't open in a web browser window. For example, some links automatically download, such as links to PDF files or Microsoft Word documents or other types of files that can't be displayed by a web browser.

To save other types of links that aren't automatically downloaded, long-press the link and choose the command Save Link from the menu that appears. If the Save Link command doesn't appear, the Galaxy Tab is unable to save the file, either because the file is of an unrecognized type or because there could be a security issue.

You can view the saved file by using the Downloads app. See the next section.

Reviewing your downloads

The Internet app keeps a list of all the stuff you download from the web. To review your download history, open the Downloads app on the Apps Menu screen. You'll see the list of downloads sorted by date, as shown in Figure 7-5.

Internet downloads	Other downloads

^ Older

	12C31568.pdf mail.cdaid.org Complete 75.44KB	9/25/2012
	12C31259.pdf mail.cdaid.org Complete 65.99KB	9/25/2012
	Wikipedia, the free encyclopedia /mnt/sdcard/Download/Main_Page.webarchivexml Complete 855KB	4/14/2012
	SOS CdA.pdf SOS CdA.pdf Complete 368KB	2/13/2012
	ElectionManualfortheWeb.pdf www.cityofboise.org Complete 377KB	10/23/2011
	WSJ Backs Labrador's Green Jobs Bill - Huckleberries Online - /mnt/sdcard/Download/wsj-backs-labradors-green-jobs-bill. Complete 1.15MB	10/17/2011
	2011-04-09_09-58-50_53.jpg 2011-04-09_09-58-50_53.jpg Complete 2.54MB	10/12/2011
	cover.png www.wambooli.com Complete 49.84KB	10/11/2011
	NIC-lawsuit-rev-5-22-11.pdf opencda.com	

Sort by size

Figure 7-5: The Download Manager.

To view a download, choose it from the list. The Galaxy Tab opens the appropriate app to view the download.

✔ The Download Manager also lists any web pages you've downloaded.

✔ To remove an item from the Downloads list, place a green check mark in its box. Touch the Trash icon at the top of the screen to remove that download.

Browser Controls and Settings

More options and settings and controls exist for the Internet app than just about any other app I've used on the Galaxy Tab. It's complex. Rather than bore you with every dang doodle detail, I thought I'd present just a few of the options worthy of your attention.

Setting a home page

The *home page* is the first page you see when you start the Internet app, and it's the first page that's loaded when you fire up a new tab. To set your home page, heed these directions:

1. **Browse to the page you want to set as the home page.**

2. **Touch the Menu icon button.**

3. **Choose Settings.**

4. **Choose General on the left side of the Settings screen.**

5. **Choose Set Home Page.**

   The Set Home Page menu appears.

6. **Touch the Current Page button.**

   The home page is set.

 If you want your home page to be blank (not set to any particular web page), choose the Blank Page item from the Set Home Page menu. I prefer a blank home page because it's the fastest web page to load. It's also the web page with the most accurate information.

Changing the way the web looks

You can do a few things to improve the way the web looks on your Galaxy Tab. First and foremost, don't forget that you can orient the device horizontally or vertically, which rearranges the way a web page is displayed.

From the Settings screen, you can also adjust the zoom setting used to display a web page. Heed these steps when using the Internet app:

1. **Touch the Menu icon button.**
2. **Choose Settings.**
3. **Choose Advanced from the left side of the screen.**
4. **On the right side of the screen, choose Default Zoom.**
5. **Choose a setting.**

   There are three options: Far, Medium, and Close for tiny, normal, and larger sized web pages, respectively.

The Close setting might not be "big" enough, so remember that you can spread your fingers to zoom in on any web page.

You can also choose the Text Size command from the Accessibility screen. That command changes the way text appears on a web page. There are five settings: Tiny through Huge.

Setting privacy and security options

With regard to security, my advice is always to be smart and think before doing anything questionable on the web. Use common sense. One of the most effective ways that the Bad Guys win is by using *human engineering* to try to trick you into doing something you normally wouldn't do, such as click a link to see a cute animation or a racy picture of a celebrity or politician. As long as you use your noggin, you should be safe.

As far as the Galaxy Tab's browser settings go, most of the security options are already enabled for you, including the blocking of pop-up windows (which normally spew ads).

If web page cookies concern you, you can clear them from the Settings window. Follow Steps 1 and 2 in the preceding section and choose Privacy & Security from the left side of the screen. Touch the option Clear All Cookie Data.

You can also choose the command Clear Form Data and remove the check mark from Remember Forum Data. These two settings prevent any text you've typed into a text field from being summoned automatically by someone who may steal your Tab.

You might be concerned about various warnings regarding location data. What they mean is that the Galaxy Tab can take advantage of your location on Planet Earth (using the GPS or satellite positioning system) to help locate businesses and people near you. I see no security problem in leaving that feature on, though you can disable location services from the Internet app's Settings screen on the Privacy & Security page: Remove the check mark by Enable Location. You can also choose the item Clear Location Access to wipe out any information saved in the Tab and used by certain web pages.

8

Chatting with Google Talk

. . . .

In This Chapter

▶ Setting up Google Talk

▶ Adding friends to the Talk app

▶ Doing a video chat

. . . .

*W*hat's the point of having a front-facing camera unless you can do video chat? Sure, you can take pictures of yourself (self-portraits). But video chat is the new rage on mobile devices.

To answer the video chat call, you run the Google Talk app. It's rather limited in that you can video (and text) chat only with your Google contacts who've also configured Google Chat, but hey: That's good enough for me!

Google Talk started out as an extension of Gmail on the Internet, primarily as a way to instantly text chat with your Google friends. Eventually they added video chat and, lo, over all these years, video chat is now available on the Galaxy Tab.

Using Google Talk

Get started with Google Talk by starting the Talk app on your Galaxy Tab. Like all the apps, it's located on the Apps Menu, though you may be lucky and find a Talk app shortcut right on the main Home screen.

When you start the Talk app the first time, you're prompted to sign in using your Google account: Touch the Sign In button. That's it for the not-quite-painful setup.

After signing in, you see the main Talk screen, shown in Figure 8-1. Your Google contacts who have activated Google Talk, either on their computer or on a mobile gizmo like the Galaxy Tab, appear on the left side of the screen.

Available friends   Set your status

Status   Invite friends

Friends list

Figure 8-1: Google Talk.

You can do three things with your friends while using the Talk app: text chat, voice chat, and video chat. But before you do any of that, you need to get some friends, as described in the next section

To sign out of Google Talk, touch the Menu icon button in the upper-right corner of the screen. Choose Sign Out from the menu.

✔ You can redisplay your account Status by choosing your account from the Friends list, such as my account being chosen in Figure 8-1.

✔ You can touch the gray Status Message box to type in a new status for your account. For example, when I was writing this book, my status was, "I'm writing a book!

Please chat with me!" Though that status wasn't very effective.

✔ Set your status icon by touching the menu just below the gray Status Message box. There are three status icons: Available, Busy, and Invisible.

Getting Friends on Google Talk

Yeah, it happens: You don't have any friends. Well, at least you don't have any friends showing up in the Friends list in Google Talk. You can easily fix that problem: Touch the Invite Friends button, as shown in Figure 8-1. Type the friend's e-mail address and touch the Done button to send that person an invite.

You'll receive a reply to your invitation on a mobile device running the Talk app or on a computer with the Gmail web page open. When you receive the invitation, you find it listed in the Friends list. Initiations have the heading Chat Invitation.

To accept an incoming invitation, touch the Chat Invitation item in your Friends list. You see the Accept Invitation dialog box. Touch the Accept button to confirm your friendship and, eventually, chat with that person.

Your friends can be on a computer or mobile device to use Google Talk; it doesn't matter which. But they must have a camera available to enable video chat.

Typing at Your Friends

The most basic form of communications with the Talk app is text chatting. That means typing at another person, which is probably one of the oldest forms of communications on the Internet. It's also the most tedious, so I'll be brief.

You start text chatting by touching a contact in the Friends list. Type your message as shown in Figure 8-2. Touch the Send button to send your comment.

You type, your friend types, and so on until you get tired or the Tab runs out of battery juice.

When you're done talking, choose another friend from the list and chat with him, or you can touch your own name on the list, which shows your current status.

Conversation   Video chat

Current chat friend   Send message   Voice chat

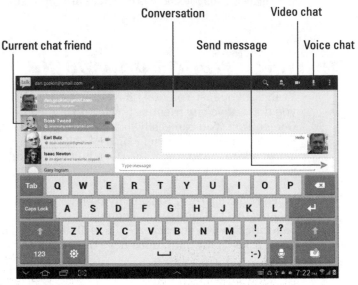

Figure 8-2: Text chatting.

Resume any conversation by choosing that same contact from the Friends list.

Talking and Video Chat

Take the conversation up a notch by touching the Voice or Video button on the right side of the text chat window. (Refer to Figure 8-2.) When you do, your friend receives an invite pop-up and Talk notification. Or if a friend is asking you to voice or video chat, you see the pop-up. Touch the Accept button to begin talking.

Figure 8-3 shows a video chat. The person you're talking with appears in the big window; you're in the smaller window. With the connection made and the invite accepted, you can begin enjoying video chat.

Connecting to the world with Skype

Perhaps the most versatile app for converting the phoneless Galaxy Tab into a phone is Skype. It's one of the most popular Internet communications programs, allowing you to text, voice, or video chat with others on the Internet as well as use the Internet to make real, honest-to-goodness phone calls.

Your Galaxy Tab doesn't come with Skype software preinstalled. To get Skype, saunter on over to the Google Play Store and download the app. (See Chapter 9 for more on the Google Play Store.)

The controls in the upper-right corner of the screen may vanish after a second; touch the screen to see the controls again.

— End video chat
— Mute the microphone
— Enter text chat
— Switch cameras

— Person you're calling

— Camera steady control

— You (and eavesdropper)

Figure 8-3: Video chat on the Galaxy Tab.

To end the conversation, touch the X (Close) button. Well, say "Goodbye" first and then touch the X button.

✔ When you're nude or just don't want to video chat, touch the Decline button for the video chat invite. Then choose that contact and reply with a text message or voice chat instead.

✔ You can disable incoming voice and video chats by deselecting the Allow Video and Voice Chats item on your Talk account's Status screen. Refer to Figure 8-1.

✔ The Galaxy Tab's front-facing camera is at the top center of the Tab. If you want to make eye contact, look directly into the camera, though when you do you won't be able to see the other person.

9

A Galaxy of Apps

*W*ithout apps, your Galaxy Tab would be nothing more than a pricey frame without a picture. There must be apps!

A moderate assortment of apps was preinstalled by Samsung, and perhaps another few apps were installed by your cellular provider. Beyond that, you can add more apps to your Tab, which extends the list of things you can do in the mobile universe. Adding new apps and managing all your Tab's apps are the topics of this chapter.

Welcome to the Play Store

People love to shop when they're buying something they want or when they're spending someone else's money. You can go shopping for your Galaxy Tab, and I'm not talking about going back to your local Phone Store to buy overpriced accessories. I'm talking about software, programs, applications — or just plain old apps.

The Google Play Store may sound like the place where you can go buy outdoor wear for children, but it's really an online place where you go to pick up new apps, buy books, and rent movies for your Galaxy Tab. You can browse, you can get free apps or books, or you can pay. It all happens at the Play Store.

- ✔ Officially, it's called the Google Play Store, but the name of the app is Play Store. It was once known as the Android Market, and you may still see it referred to as the Market.

- ✔ *App* is short for application. It's a program, or software, you can add to your Galaxy Tab to make it do new, wondrous, or useful things.

- ✔ Because the Galaxy Tab uses the Android operating system, it can run nearly all apps written for Android.

- ✔ You can be assured that all apps that appear in the Google Play Store can be used with the Galaxy Tab. There's no way to download or buy something that's incompatible with your Tab.

- ✔ All apps you download can be found on the Apps Menu screen. Further, apps you download have shortcut icons placed on the Home screen.

- ✔ You obtain items from the Google Play Store by *downloading* them into your Tab. That file transfer works best at top speeds; therefore:

- ✔ I highly recommend that you connect your cellular Tab to a Wi-Fi network if you plan to obtain apps, books, or movies at the Google Play Store. Not only does Wi-Fi give you speed, but it also helps avoid data surcharges. See Chapter 10 for details on connecting the Galaxy Tab to a Wi-Fi network.

Browsing the Google Play Store

You access the Google Play Store by opening the Play Store app, found on the Apps Menu screen but also on the main Home screen.

After opening the Play Store app, you see the main screen, similar to the one shown in Figure 9-1. You can browse for apps, games, books, or movie rentals. The categories are listed on the top-right part of the screen, with the other parts of the screen highlighting popular or recommended items. Those recommendations are color-coded to let you know what they are: green for apps, orange for music, cyan for books, blue for magazines, and red for video rentals.

Go to the main screen   My Apps Search for apps

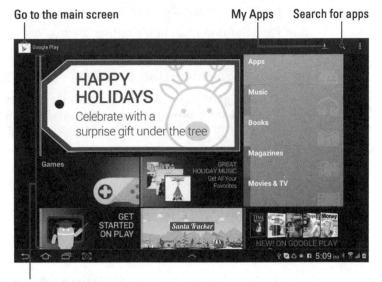

Recommendations

Figure 9-1: The Google Play Store.

Find apps by choosing the Apps category from the main screen. (Refer to Figure 9-1.) The next screen lists popular and featured items plus categories you can browse by swiping the screen right to left. The category titles appear toward the top of the screen.

When you have an idea of what you want, such as an app's name or even what it does, searching works fastest: Touch the Search button at the top of the Play Store screen. (Refer to Figure 9-1.) Type all or part of the app's name or perhaps a description.

To see more information about an item, touch it. Touching something doesn't buy it but instead displays a more detailed description, screen shots, a video preview, comments, plus links to similar items.

Return to the main Google Play Store screen at any time by touching the Google Play icon in the upper-left corner of the screen.

- ✔ The first time you enter the Google Play Store, or after the Play Store app is updated, you have to accept the terms of service; touch the Accept button.

- ✔ Pay attention to an app's ratings. Ratings are added by people who use the apps — people like you and me. Having more stars is better. You can see additional information, including individual user reviews, by choosing the app.

- ✔ Another good indicator of an app's success is how many times it's been downloaded. Some apps have been downloaded over ten million times. That's a good sign.

- ✔ Apps you download are added to the Apps Menu, made available like any other app on your Tab.

Getting a free app

After you locate an app you want, the next step is to download it. Follow these steps:

1. **If possible, activate the Wi-Fi connection to avoid incurring data overages.**

   See Chapter 10 for information on connecting your Galaxy Tab to a Wi-Fi network.

2. **Open the Play Store app.**

3. **Locate the app you want and open its description.**

   You can browse for apps or use the Search button to find an app by name or what it does.

4. **Touch the Install button.**

   Free apps feature an Install button. Paid apps have a button with the app's price on it. (See the next section for information on buying an app.)

   After touching the Install button, you're alerted to any services that the app uses. The list of permissions isn't a warning, and it doesn't mean anything bad. It's just that the Play Store is telling you which of your Tab's features the app uses.

5. **Touch the Accept & Download button to accept the conditions and begin the download.**

6. **Touch the Open button to run the app.**

Or, if you were doing something else while the app was downloading and installing, choose the Installed App notification, as shown in the margin. The notification features the app's name with the text `Successfully Installed` beneath it.

At this point, what happens next depends on the app you've downloaded. For example, you may have to agree to a license agreement. If so, touch the I Agree button. Additional setup may involve setting your location, signing in to an account, or creating a profile, for example.

After you complete the initial setup, or if no setup is necessary, you can start using the app.

Chapter 12 lists some Android apps that I recommend, all of which are free.

Buying an app

Some great free apps are available, but many of the apps you dearly want probably cost money. It's not a lot of money, especially compared with the price of computer software. In fact, it seems odd to sit and stew over whether paying 99 cents for a game is "worth it."

I recommend that you download a free app first to familiarize yourself with the process.

When you're ready to pay for an app, follow these steps:

1. **Activate the Galaxy Tab's Wi-Fi connection.**

2. **Open the Play Store app.**

3. **Browse or search for the app you want and then choose the app to display its description.**

4. **Touch the Price button.**

The Price button lists the app's price, such as $0.99.

The next window displays the services the app uses, such as Storage to keep high scores or other data, Networking Communication to access the Internet, and so on.

5. **Choose your payment method.**

Account balance and credit card information appears at the top of the Purchase window. The card must be on file with Google Checkout. If you don't yet have a card on file, choose the option Add Card and then fill in the fields on the Credit Card screen to add your payment method to Google Checkout.

6. **Touch the Accept & Buy button.**

Your payment method is authorized, and the app is downloaded and installed.

The app can be accessed from the Apps Menu, just like all other apps available on your Galaxy Tab. Or if you're still at the app's screen in the Play Store, touch the Open button.

Eventually, you receive an e-mail message from the Google Play Store, confirming your purchase. The message contains a link you can click to review the refund policy should you change your mind on the purchase.

Be quick on that refund: Some apps allow you only 15 minutes to get your money back. Otherwise, the standard refund period is 24 hours. You know when the time is up because the Refund button changes its name to Uninstall.

Also see the section "Removing downloaded apps," later in this chapter.

App Management 101

The Play Store is not only where you buy apps — it's also the place you return to for performing app management. That task includes reviewing apps you've downloaded, updating apps, organizing apps, and removing apps you no longer want or that you severely hate.

Reviewing your apps

To peruse the apps you've downloaded from the Google Play Store, follow these steps:

1. **Start the Play Store app.**

2. **Choose My Apps from the top of the screen.**

3. **Peruse your apps.**

There are two categories for your Play Store apps: Installed and All, as shown in Figure 9-2. Installed apps are found on your Tab; All apps include apps you have downloaded but which may not currently be installed.

Apps in need of an update Automatic updating Manual update

Apps Installed Update apps Remove app

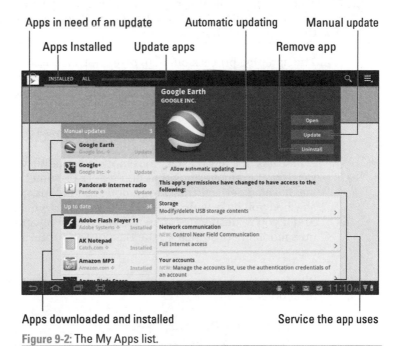

Apps downloaded and installed   Service the app uses

Figure 9-2: The My Apps list.

Touch an app to see details about the app, such as the details for Google Earth, shown in Figure 9-2. Touch the Open button to run the app, the Update button to update to the latest version, or the Uninstall button to remove the app. Later sections in this chapter describe the details on updating and uninstalling apps.

Updating an app

One nice thing about using the Google Play Store to get new software is that the Play Store also notifies you of new versions of the apps you download. Whenever a new version of any app is available, you see it flagged for updating, as shown in Figure 9-2. Updating the app to get the latest version is cinchy.

Some apps are updated automatically; there's no need for you to do anything. Other apps (refer to Figure 9-2) must be updated individually. To do so, touch the Update button for the app (as illustrated in Figure 9-2) to manually update it.

To make updating easier, you can place a green check mark by the item Allow Automatic Updating. Refer to Figure 9-2 for that check mark box's location.

The updating process often involves downloading and installing a new version of the app. That's perfectly fine; your settings and options aren't changed by the update process.

Removing downloaded apps

I can think of a few reasons to remove an app. It's with eager relish that I remove apps that don't work or somehow annoy me. It's also perfectly okay to remove redundant apps, such as when you have multiple eBook readers that you don't use. And if you're desperate for an excuse, removing apps frees up a modicum of storage in the Galaxy Tab's internal storage area.

Whatever the reason, remove an app by following these directions:

1. **Start the Play Store app.**
2. **Choose My Apps from the top of the screen.**
3. **In the Installed list, touch the app that offends you.**
4. **Touch the Uninstall button.**
5. **Touch the OK button to confirm.**

   The app is removed.

The app continues to appear on the All list even after it's been removed. (After all, you downloaded it once.) That doesn't mean that the app is installed.

✔ You can always reinstall paid apps that you've uninstalled. You aren't charged twice for doing so.

✔ You can't remove apps that are preinstalled on the Tab by either Samsung or your cellular service provider. I'm sure there's probably a technical way to uninstall the apps, but seriously: Just don't use the apps if you want to remove them and discover that you can't.

10

It's a Wireless Life

*W*hat exactly is *portable?* Back in the olden days, the boys in Marketing would say that bolting a handle to just about anything made it portable. Even a rhinoceros would be portable if he had a handle. Well, and the legs, they kind of make the rhino portable, I suppose. But my point is that to be portable requires more than just a handle; it requires a complete lack of wires.

The Galaxy Tab's battery keeps it away from a wall socket. The digital cellular signal keeps your gizmo away from a phone line. Other types of wireless communications are available to the Tab, including Wi-Fi and Bluetooth. Both of those features ensure the Tab's portability, and they're both covered in this chapter.

Wireless Networking Wizardry

You know that wireless networking has hit the big-time when you see people asking Santa Claus for a wireless router at Christmas. Such a thing would have been unheard of years ago because routers were used primarily for woodworking back then. Today, wireless networking is what keeps gizmos like the Galaxy Tab connected to the Internet.

The primary reason for wireless networking on the Galaxy Tab is to connect to the Internet. For exchanging and synchronizing files, refer to Chapter 11.

Using the cellular data network

The cellular Galaxy Tab is designed to connect to the Internet by using the digital cellular network. This signal is the same type used by cell phones and cellular modems to wirelessly connect to the Internet.

Several types of digital cellular networks are available:

4G LTE/HSPA: The fourth generation of wide-area data networks is as much as ten times faster than the 3G network and is the latest craze in cellular networking. The cellular providers are busily covering the country in a coat of 4G LTE or HSPA paint; if the signal isn't available in your area now, it will be soon.

3G: The third generation of wide-area data networks is several times faster than the previous generation of data networks. This type of wireless signal is the most popular in the United States.

1X: There are several types of original, slower cellular data signals available. They all fall under the 1X banner. It's slow.

Your Galaxy Tab always uses the best network available. So, if the 4G LTE network is within reach, that network is used for Internet communications. Otherwise, a slower network is chosen.

✔ A notification icon for the type of network being used appears in the status area, right next to the Signal Strength icon.

✔ Accessing the digital cellular network isn't free. Your Galaxy Tab most likely has some form of subscription plan for a certain quantity of data. When you exceed that quantity, the costs can become prohibitive.

✔ A better way to connect your Galaxy Tab to the Internet is to use the Wi-Fi signal, covered in the next section. The digital cellular network signal makes for a great fallback because it's available in more places than Wi-Fi is.

✔ Wi-Fi–only Galaxy Tabs can't access the digital cellular network.

Understanding Wi-Fi

The digital cellular connection is nice, and it's available pretty much all over, but it will cost you moolah. A better option, and one you should seek out when it's available, is *Wi-Fi*, or the same wireless networking standard used by computers for communicating with each other and the Internet.

To make Wi-Fi work on the Galaxy Tab requires two steps. First, you must activate Wi-Fi, by turning on the Tab's wireless radio. The second step, covered in the following section, is connecting to a specific wireless network.

Activating and deactivating Wi-Fi

Follow these carefully written directions to activate Wi-Fi networking on your Galaxy Tab:

1. **Touch the Apps Menu button.**

2. **Open the Settings app.**

3. **Choose the Wi-Fi item.**

   The Wi-Fi window appears on the right side of the screen.

4. **Slide the button by the Wi-Fi item to the right.**

   When the button is green, Wi-Fi is on.

After the Tab's Wi-Fi radio is activated, you can connect the tablet to a Wi-Fi network. If you've already configured your Tab to connect to an available wireless network, it's connected automatically. Otherwise, you have to connect to an available network, which is covered in the next section.

To turn off Wi-Fi, slide the button by the Wi-Fi option to the left (Step 4). Turning off Wi-Fi disconnects the Tab from any wireless networks.

> ✔ If you place a check mark by the option Notify Me on the Wi-Fi window, the Tab alerts you to the presence of available Wi-Fi networks whenever you're in range and not connected to a network. This option is a good one to have set when you're frequently on the road. That's because:

> ✔ Using Wi-Fi to connect to the Internet doesn't incur data usage charges.

> ✔ The Galaxy Tab Wi-Fi radio places an extra drain on the battery, but it's truly negligible. If you want to save a modicum of juice, especially if you're out and about and don't plan to be near a Wi-Fi access point for any length of time, turn off the Wi-Fi radio as described in this section.

Connecting to a Wi-Fi network

After you've activated the Galaxy Tab's Wi-Fi radio, you can connect to an available wireless network. Heed these steps:

1. **Touch the Apps Menu button on the Home screen.**

2. **Open the Settings app.**

3. **Choose Wi-Fi.**

4. **Ensure that Wi-Fi is on.**

    When the button turns green, Wi-Fi is on.

5. **Choose a wireless network from the list.**

    Available Wi-Fi networks appear at the bottom of the screen, as shown in Figure 10-1. When no wireless networks are listed, you're sort of out of luck regarding wireless access from your current location.

    In Figure 10-1, I chose the Imperial Wambooli network, which is my office network.

Wi-Fi radio is on   Manually connect

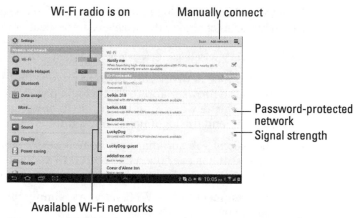

Password-protected
network

Signal strength

Available Wi-Fi networks

Figure 10-1: Finding a wireless network.

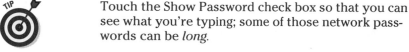

6. **Optionally, type the network password.**

   Touch the Password text box to see the onscreen keyboard.

   Touch the Show Password check box so that you can see what you're typing; some of those network passwords can be *long*.

7. **Touch the Connect button.**

   You should be immediately connected to the network. If not, try the password again.

When the Galaxy Tab is connected to a wireless network, you see the Wi-Fi status icon, shown in the margin. This icon replaces the cellular data signal icon. It means that the Tab's Wi-Fi is on, connected, and communicating with a Wi-Fi network.

Some wireless networks don't broadcast their names, which adds security but also makes connecting more difficult. In those cases, touch the Add Network button (refer to Figure 10-1) to manually add the network. You need to type the network name, or *SSID,* and choose the type of security. You also need the password if one is used. You can obtain this information from the girl with the pink hair who sold you coffee or from whomever is in charge of the wireless network at your location.

- ✔ Not every wireless network has a password.

- ✔ Some public networks are open to anyone, but you have to use the Browser app to find a login page that lets you access the network: Simply browse to any page on the Internet, and the login page shows up.

- ✔ The Galaxy Tab automatically remembers every Wi-Fi network it has ever been connected to and automatically reconnects upon finding the same network again.

- ✔ To disconnect from a Wi-Fi network, simply turn off Wi-Fi. See the preceding section.

- ✔ Unlike a cellular data network, a Wi-Fi network's broadcast signal goes only so far. My advice is to use Wi-Fi whenever you plan to remain in one location for a while. If you wander too far away, your Tab loses the signal and is disconnected.

A Connection Shared

Your Galaxy Tab has no trouble sniffing out a digital cellular signal, so it can access the Internet just about anywhere. Your laptop might not be so lucky. But hey: You're already paying for the digital cellular signal, right? So why should you bother getting a digital cellular modem for the laptop, as well as buying into another cellular contract, when you could just use the Galaxy Tab as a portable modem?

Sharing the Galaxy Tab's Internet connection is not only possible, but also relatively easy. You can go about sharing in one of two ways: The wireless way is to create a mobile hotspot; the wired way is to use the *tethering* technique. Both methods are covered in this section.

Creating a mobile hotspot

You can direct the Galaxy Tab to share its digital cellular connection with as many as five other wireless gizmos. This process is referred to as *creating a mobile, wireless hotspot,* though no heat or fire is involved.

To set up a mobile hotspot with your Galaxy Tab, heed these steps:

1. **Turn off the Galaxy Tab's Wi-Fi radio.**

   You can't be using a Wi-Fi connection when you create a Wi-Fi hotspot. Actually, the notion is kind of silly: If the Galaxy Tab can get a Wi-Fi signal, other gizmos can too, so why bother creating a Wi-Fi hotspot in the first place?

   See the earlier section, "Activating and deactivating Wi-Fi," for information on disabling Wi-Fi on your Galaxy Tab.

2. **If you can, plug in the Galaxy Tab.**

   It's okay if you don't find a power outlet, but running a mobile hotspot draws a lot of power. The Tab's battery power drains quickly if you can't plug in.

3. **From the Apps screen, open the Settings app.**

   Touch the Apps Menu button to get to the Apps screen.

4. **Choose Mobile Hotspot.**

   The Mobile Hotspot window appears on the right side of the screen.

5. **Slide the Mobile Hotspot button to the right.**

   The button turns green when the Mobile Hotspot feature is active.

 When the hotspot is activated, you see the Tethering or Hotspot Active status icon displayed, similar to what's shown in the margin. You can continue to use the Galaxy Tab while it's sharing the digital cellular connection, but other devices can now use their Wi-Fi radio to access your Tab's shared connection.

To turn off the mobile hotspot, slide the Mobile Hotspot button to the left (Step 5).

▱ You can change the mobile hotspot configuration by touching the Configure button at the top of the Mobile Hotspot window.

▱ The range for the mobile hotspot is about 30 feet.

▱ Some cellular providers may not allow you to create a mobile hotspot, and of course, you cannot create a mobile hotspot when your Galaxy Tab doesn't use the cellular data network.

▱ Don't forget to turn off the mobile hotspot when you're done using it. Those data rates can certainly add up!

Sharing the Internet via tethering

Another, more personal way to share your Galaxy Tab's digital cellular connection, and to get one other device on the Internet, is *tethering*. This operation is carried out by connecting the Tab to another gizmo, such as a laptop computer, via its USB cable. Then you activate USB tethering, and the other gizmo is suddenly using the Galaxy Tab like a modem.

To set up tethering on your Galaxy Tab, heed these directions:

1. **Turn off the Tab's Wi-Fi radio.**

   You cannot share a connection with the Wi-Fi radio on; you can share only the digital cellular connection.

2. **Connect the Tab to a PC using its USB cable.**

   Specifically, the PC must be running Windows or some flavor of the Linux operating system.

3. **At the Home screen, touch the Apps Menu button.**

4. **Open the Settings app.**

5. **Touch the More button, found beneath the Data Usage button.**

6. **Choose Tethering.**

7. **Place a green check mark by the option USB Tethering.**

8. **On the PC, choose Public when prompted to specify the type of network to which you've just connected.**

Though the Galaxy Tab's digital cellular network is being shared, you see the Tethering Active notification, shown in the margin. You can choose that notification to turn off tethering: Simply remove the check mark by the USB Tethering option.

    ✒ Sharing the digital network connection incurs data usage charges against your cellular data plan. Be careful with your data usage when you're sharing a connection.

   ✒ You may be prompted on the PC to locate and install software for the Galaxy Tab. Do so: Accept the installation of new software when prompted by Windows.

The Bluetooth Experience

Computer nerds have long had the desire to connect high-tech gizmos to one another. The Bluetooth standard was developed to sate this desire in a wireless way. Though Bluetooth is wireless communication, it's not the same as wireless networking. It's more about connecting peripheral devices, such as keyboards, mice, printers, headphones, and other gear. It all happens in a wireless way, as described in this section.

Understanding Bluetooth

Bluetooth is a peculiar name for a wireless communications standard. Unlike Wi-Fi networking, with Bluetooth you simply connect two gizmos. Here's how the operation works:

1. **Turn on the Bluetooth wireless radio on each gizmo.**

   There are two Bluetooth gizmos: the peripheral and the main device to which you're connecting the gizmo, such as the Galaxy Tab.

2. **Make the gizmo you're trying to connect to discoverable.**

   By making a device discoverable, you're telling it to send a signal to other Bluetooth gizmos, saying, "Here I am!"

3. On the Galaxy Tab, choose the peripheral gizmo from the list of Bluetooth devices.

This action is known as *pairing* the devices.

4. Optionally, confirm the connection on the peripheral device.

For example, you may be asked to input a code or press a button.

5. Use the device.

What you can do with the device depends on what it does.

When you're done using the device, you simply turn it off. Because the Bluetooth gizmo is paired with the Galaxy Tab, it's automatically reconnected the next time you turn it on (that is, if you have Bluetooth activated on the Tab).

 Bluetooth devices are marked with the Bluetooth icon, shown in the margin. It's your assurance that the gizmo can work with other Bluetooth devices.

Activating Bluetooth

To make the Bluetooth connection, you turn on the Galaxy Tab's Bluetooth radio. Obey these directions:

1. On the Apps screen, open the Settings icon.

2. Choose Bluetooth.

3. Slide the button by the Bluetooth option to the right.

The button turns green when Bluetooth is on.

 When Bluetooth is on, the Bluetooth status icon appears, as shown in the margin.

To turn off Bluetooth, repeat the steps in this section: Slide the button to the left in Step 3.

 From the And-Now-He-Tells-Us Department, you can quickly activate Bluetooth by using the Quick Actions on the Notification shade: Touch the time display on your Galaxy

Tab to pop up the Notification panel. Slide the Quick Actions over to the left and touch the Bluetooth button. Likewise, you can deactivate Bluetooth by touching the button a second time.

Connecting to a Bluetooth device

To make the Bluetooth connection between the Galaxy Tab and some other gizmo, follow these steps:

1. **Ensure that Bluetooth is on.**

   Refer to the preceding section.

2. **Turn on the Bluetooth gizmo or ensure that its Bluetooth radio is on.**

   Some Bluetooth devices have separate power and Bluetooth switches.

3. **On the Galaxy Tab, touch the Apps Menu button on the Home screen and run the Settings app.**

4. **Choose Bluetooth.**

   The Bluetooth Settings window appears.

5. **If the other device has an option to become visible, select it.**

   For example, some Bluetooth gizmos have a tiny button to press that makes the device visible to other Bluetooth gizmos. (You don't need to make the Galaxy Tab visible unless you're accessing it from another Bluetooth gizmo.)

6. **Choose Scan for Devices.**

   Eventually, the device should appear on the Bluetooth Settings window, as shown in Figure 10-2.

7. **Choose the device.**

   For example, the Photosmart Premium printer, shown in Figure 10-2.

Bluetooth is on   Check for Bluetooth gizmos

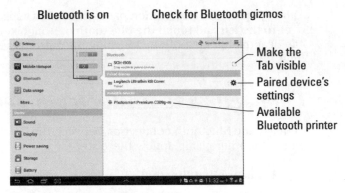

Make the
Tab visible

Paired device's
settings

Available
Bluetooth printer

Figure 10-2: Finding Bluetooth gizmos.

8. If necessary, input the device's passcode or otherwise acknowledge the connection.

Not every device has a passcode. If prompted, acknowledge the passcode on either the Galaxy Tab or the other device.

After you acknowledge the passcode (or not), the Bluetooth gizmo and your Galaxy Tab are connected and communicating. You can begin using the device.

Connected devices appear on the Bluetooth Settings window, under the heading Paired Devices.

To break the connection, you can either turn off the gizmo or disable the Bluetooth radio on your Galaxy Tab. Because the devices are paired, when you turn on Bluetooth and reactivate the device, the connection is instantly reestablished.

✔ You can unpair a device by touching the gear icon next to the device in the Bluetooth Settings window (refer to Figure 10-2). Choose the Unpair command to break the Bluetooth connection and stop using the device.

✔ Only unpair devices you don't plan on using again in the future. Otherwise, simply turn off the Bluetooth device.

✔ Bluetooth can use a lot of power. Especially for battery-powered devices, don't forget to turn them off when you're no longer using them with the Galaxy Tab.

11

Connect, Share, and Store

In This Chapter

▶ Making the USB connection

▶ Moving files between a PC and the Tab

▶ Transferring files with Bluetooth

▶ Synchronizing media with doubleTwist

▶ Performing basic file management

*T*he Galaxy Tab is adept at communicating wirelessly. It can connect to the Internet using the digital cellular signal or over a Wi-Fi connection. Beyond that, you can use the USB cable to connect your Tab to another gizmo. No, you cannot use the USB cable to connect the Galaxy Tab to the couch, or the toaster, or the time machine. You can, however, use the USB cable to connect the Galaxy Tab to a computer. This chapter describes all the wonderful things that can happen after you make that connection.

The USB Connection

The most direct way to connect a Galaxy Tab to a computer is by using a wire — specifically, the wire nestled cozily in the heart of a USB cable. There are lots of things you can do after making the USB connection. Before doing those things, you need to connect the cable.

Yeah, it may seem excessive to write an entire section on what's apparently a simple operation. But if you've used the Galaxy Tab and already tried to make a USB connection, you probably discovered that it's not so simple.

Connecting the Tab to your PC

The USB connection between the Galaxy Tab and your computer works fastest when both devices are physically connected. You make this connection happen by using the USB cable that comes with the Tab. Like nearly every computer cable in the Third Dimension, the USB cable has two ends:

- The A end of the USB cable plugs into the computer.
- The other end of the cable plugs into the bottom of the Galaxy Tab.

The connectors are shaped differently and cannot be plugged in either backward or upside down. (The end that inserts into the Galaxy Tab has the *SAMSUNG* text facing you when you plug it in.)

After you understand how the cable works, plug the USB cable into one of the computer's USB ports. Then plug the USB cable into the Galaxy Tab.

- As far as I can tell, you cannot connect the Galaxy Tab to a Macintosh and have it be recognized as an external storage device or media player.
- You can, however, use Bluetooth to send and receive files between the Galaxy Tab and a Mac. It's not the fastest way to exchange information, but it works. See the later section, "Using Bluetooth to copy a file."

Dealing with the USB connection

Upon making the USB connection between the Galaxy Tab and a PC, a number of things happen. Don't let any of these things cause you undue alarm.

First, you may see the MTP application screen appear on the Galaxy Tab. That screen indicates that the Tab is actively looking for the Samsung Kies program, which it can use to automatically synchronize information between the Tab and your PC.

Second, you may see some activity on the PC, some drivers being installed and such. That's normal behavior any time you first connect a new USB gizmo to a Windows computer.

Third, you may witness the AutoPlay dialog box. That dialog box helps you deal with the Galaxy Tab connection, to transfer music, pictures, files, and so on.

Choose an option from the AutoPlay dialog box, such as Sync Digital Media Files to This Device. From that point on, you'll use Windows or a program on your computer to work with the files on your Galaxy Tab.

Don't be surprised if the AutoPlay dialog box doesn't appear; many PCs are configured to ignore new gizmos. That's okay: You can always manually summon the various options displayed in the AutoPlay dialog box, as discussed elsewhere in this chapter.

Fourth, the Galaxy Tab is added to your computer's storage system. You see it listed as a device in the Computer window. On my PC, the Tab is assumed to be a portable music player; its icon is shown in the margin.

Bottom line: When you make the USB connection, you can exchange information between your computer and the Galaxy Tab.

   ✔ When the Galaxy Tab is connected to a computer using the USB connection, the USB notification appears at the bottom of the screen, as shown in the margin. Choosing that notification does nothing.

   ✔ For the Apple Macintosh computer, obtain a copy of the Android File Transfer program to help move files between the Mac and Tab at `www.android.com/ filetransfer`.

Disconnecting the Tab from your computer

This process is cinchy: When you're done transferring files, music, or other media between your PC and the Tab, close all the programs and folders you have opened on the PC, specifically those you've used to work with the Tab's storage. Then you can disconnect the USB cable. That's it.

On a Mac, eject the Tab's storage before you disconnect the USB cable: Drag the storage icons to the Trash or, in any Finder window, click the Eject button by the storage icons.

To be safe, close those programs and folder windows you've opened before disconnecting the Tab.

Files from Here, Files to There

The point of making the USB connection between your Galaxy Tab and the computer is to exchange files. You can't just wish the files over. Instead, I recommend following the advice in this section, which also covers transferring files using Bluetooth.

A good understanding of basic file operations is necessary before you attempt file transfers between your computer and the Galaxy Tab. You need to know how to copy, move, rename, and delete files. It also helps to be familiar with what folders are and how they work.

Transferring files to the Tab

There are plenty of reasons you would want to copy a file from your computer to the Galaxy Tab. You can copy over your pictures and videos, and you can copy over music or audio files. You can even copy vCards that you export from your e-mail program.

Follow these steps to copy a file from your computer to the Galaxy Tab:

1. **Connect the Galaxy Tab to the computer by using the USB cable.**

   Specific directions are offered earlier in this chapter.

2. **If the AutoPlay dialog box appears, choose the option Open Folder/Device to View Files. Otherwise, open the Computer window, then open the Galaxy Tab's icon, and then open the Tablet icon.**

   The AutoPlay dialog box is shown in Figure 11-1.

Figure 11-1: The AutoPlay dialog box for the Galaxy Tab.

3. **Locate the files you want to copy to the Tab.**

   Open the folder that contains the files, or somehow have the file icons visible on the screen.

4. **Drag the File icon from its folder on your computer to the Galaxy Tab window.**

   If you want to be specific, drag the file to the `download` folder; otherwise, you can place the file into the Galaxy Tab's root folder, as shown in Figure 11-2.

Specific folders on the Galaxy Tab

Drag files here to copy to the 'root'

Files on your computer

Files on the Galaxy Tab

Figure 11-2: Copying files to the Galaxy Tab.

5. **Close the folder windows and disconnect the USB cable when you're done.**

   Refer to specific instructions earlier in this chapter.

Any files you've copied are now stored on the Galaxy Tab. What you do with them next depends on the reasons you copied the files: to view pictures, use the Gallery, import vCards, use the Contacts app, listen to music, or use the Music app, for example.

The best way to move music and pictures over to your Galaxy Tab from the computer is to synchronize them. See the later section, "Synchronize with doubleTwist."

Copying files to your computer

After you've survived the ordeal of copying files from your computer to the Galaxy Tab, copying files in the other direction is a cinch: Follow the steps in the preceding section, but in Steps 3 and 4 you're dragging the File icons from the Galaxy Tab folder window to your computer.

My advice is to drag the files to your computer's desktop, unless you know of another location where you want the files copied.

Using Bluetooth to copy a file

Here's a great way to give yourself a headache: Use the Bluetooth networking system to copy a file between your Galaxy Tab and a Bluetooth-enabled computer. It's slow and painful, but it works.

Get started by pairing the Galaxy Tab with the Bluetooth computer. See Chapter 10 for details on the whole pairing-discovery thing. When your Tab and computer are paired and connected, how the file transfer works depends on whether you're using a PC or a Macintosh.

Send a file from the PC to the Galaxy Tab

On a PC, follow these steps to copy a file to the Galaxy Tab:

1. **Right-click the Bluetooth icon in the Notification Area.**

   The icon looks like the Bluetooth logo, shown in the margin. The Notification Area dwells on the far-right end of the taskbar.

2. **Choose Send a File from the pop-up menu.**

3. **Choose the Galaxy Tab from the list of Bluetooth devices.**

   If you don't see the Tab listed, ensure that the Bluetooth radio is on for both devices and that they're paired.

4. **Click the Next button.**

5. **Click the Browse button to locate files to send to the Tab.**

6. **Use the Browse dialog box to locate and select one or more files.**

7. **Click the Open button to choose the file(s).**

8. **Click the Next button.**

9. **On the Galaxy Tab, touch the Accept button to receive the file.**

   The Tab may play a notification alert, which lets you know that the file is coming over.

10. **On the PC, touch the Finish button.**

    The transfer is complete.

    ✔ Images sent to the Galaxy Tab from a PC can be found in the Gallery app, in the Bluetooth album.

    ✔ Not all PCs are equipped with Bluetooth. To add Bluetooth to a PC, you need a Bluetooth adapter. Inexpensive USB Bluetooth adapters are available at most computer and office supply stores.

Receive a file on a PC from the Galaxy Tab

To send a file from the Tab to a PC, you need to use the Bluetooth item found on the Share menu in various apps. Follow these steps:

1. **On the Galaxy Tab, locate the media or file you want to send to the PC.**

2. **Choose the Share command.**

3. **From the Share or Share Via menu, choose Bluetooth.**

   A list of Bluetooth devices appears.

4. **Choose the PC from the list.**

5. **On the PC, click the Notification Area icon that appears, indicating that a Bluetooth file transfer request is pending.**

6. **On the PC, click the OK button in the Access Authorization dialog box.**

   The file is sent to the PC.

On my PC, the received files are stored in the Bluetooth Exchange Folder, found in the Documents or My Documents folder.

Send a file from a Macintosh to the Tab

On a Macintosh, to copy a file to the Galaxy Tab by using Bluetooth, follow these steps:

1. **Use the Bluetooth menu on the Mac to choose the Galaxy Tab and then Send File, as shown in Figure 11-3.**

   You can find the Bluetooth menu at the far-right end of the menu bar. The Galaxy Tab is probably named SCH-I905, which is Samsung's super secret code name for the cellular Tab.

Galaxy Tab   Bluetooth menu

Figure 11-3: Copying a file using Bluetooth on the Mac.

2. Use the Select File to Send dialog box to browse for the file you want to send from the Mac to the Galaxy Tab.

3. On the Galaxy Tab, choose the Bluetooth notification.

4. In the dialog box that appears on the Tab, touch the Accept button to receive the file.

Sadly, I cannot get the Mac to accept a file sent to it using the Bluetooth item from the Share menu. That method may work in the future, in which case the steps should work similar to those described in the earlier section, "Receive a file on a PC from the Galaxy Tab."

Synchronize with doubleTwist

Perhaps the most effective and easy way to move information between the Galaxy Tab and your computer is to use a synchronization utility. One of the most popular is the free program doubleTwist, available at `www.doubletwist.com`.

doubleTwist isn't an Android app. You use it on your computer. It helps you synchronize pictures, music, videos, and web page subscriptions between your computer and its media libraries and any portable device, such as the Galaxy Tab. Additionally, doubleTwist gives you the ability to search the Google Play Store and obtain new apps for your tablet.

To use doubleTwist, connect the Galaxy Tab to your computer as described earlier in this chapter. Use the USB cable to make the PC-Tab connection.

If the doubleTwist program doesn't start automatically after you connect the Tab, start it manually. The doubleTwist interface is illustrated in Figure 11-4.

To best use doubleTwist, place a check mark by the items you want to sync on the General tab. (Refer to Figure 11-4.) Or, you can choose a tab, such as Videos or Pictures, as shown in Figure 11-4, to select specific items to synchronize. Click the Sync button to copy those files to the Galaxy Tab.

View local media

Items to sync

Look for apps

Choose items to sync

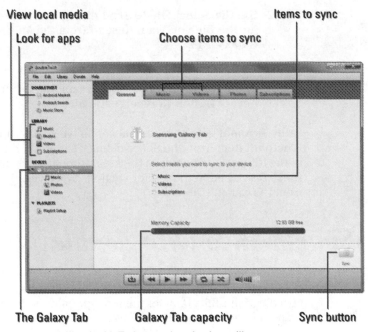

The Galaxy Tab

Galaxy Tab capacity

Sync button

Figure 11-4: The doubleTwist synchronization utility.

Another way to use doubleTwist is to copy media items to the Galaxy Tab by selecting and then dragging their icons. Choose a media category on your computer, as shown on the left side of the doubleTwist window in Figure 11-4. Drag media from your computer to the Galaxy Tab's icon to copy over those files.

Some media organization programs on your computer, such as Windows Music Player or Windows Photo Gallery, may allow you to synchronize your media with the Galaxy Tab just as well as or perhaps better than doubleTwist.

The Galaxy Tab's Storage

Somewhere, deep in the bosom of your Galaxy Tab, there lies a storage device or two. The storage in the Tab works like the hard drive in your computer. Internal storage can't be removed, only the MicroSD card storage (if your Tab is blessed with it), but that's not the point. The point is that the storage is used for your apps, music, videos, pictures, and a host of other information. This section describes what you can do to manage that storage.

Reviewing storage stats

You can see how much storage space is available on your Galaxy Tab's internal storage by following these steps:

1. **At the Home screen, touch the Apps Menu icon button.**

2. **Open the Settings app and choose Storage.**

   You see a screen similar to Figure 11-5. It details information about storage space on the Galaxy Tab's internal storage.

Figure 11-5: Galaxy Tab storage information.

You can choose a category to see more information, or to launch a program. For example, touching the Miscellaneous Files category (refer to Figure 11-5) displays a list of various apps and files you've downloaded. Touching the Pictures, Videos category starts the Gallery app.

Managing files

You probably didn't get a Galaxy Tab because you enjoy managing files on a computer and wanted another gizmo to hone your skills. Even so, you can practice the same type of file manipulation on the Tab as you would on a computer. Is there a need to do so? Of course not! But if you want to get dirty with files, you can.

The main tool for managing files is the My Files app. It's a traditional type of file management app, which means if you detest managing files on your computer, you'll experience the same pain and frustration on your Galaxy Tab. The My Files app's main screen is shown in Figure 11-6.

Create a new folder

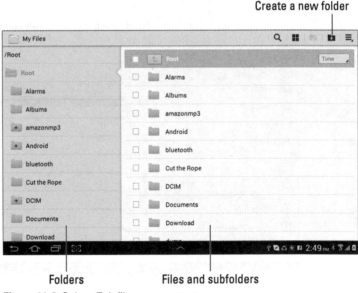

Folders   Files and subfolders

Figure 11-6: Galaxy Tab file management.

12

Ten Great Apps

*T*here are more than 100,000 apps available at the Google
Play Store — so many that it would take you more than
a relaxing evening to discover them all. Rather than list
every single app, I've culled from the lot some apps that I
find exceptional — that show the diversity of the Google Play
Store but also how well the Galaxy Tab can run Android apps.

Every app listed in this chapter is free; see Chapter 9 for
directions on finding them using the Google Play Store.

AK Notepad

One program that the Galaxy Tab is missing out of the box
is a notepad. A good choice for an app to fill that void is AK
Notepad: You can type or dictate short messages and memos,
which I find handy.

For example, before a recent visit to the hardware store, I made
(dictated) a list of items I needed by using AK Notepad. I also
keep some important items as notes — things that I often forget
or don't care to remember, such as frequent flyer numbers, my
dress shirt and suit size (like I ever need that info), and other
important notes I might need handy but not cluttering my brain.

Angry Birds

The birds may be angry at the green piggies for stealing eggs,
but you'll be crazy for this addictive game. Like most popular
games, Angry Birds is simple. It's easy to learn, fun to play.
The best part is that on the Galaxy Tab, with its awesome
10.1-inch display, the Angry Birds game is beautiful.

Gesture Search

The Gesture Search app provides a new way to find information on your Galaxy Tab. Rather than use a keyboard or dictate, you simply draw on the touchscreen the first letter of whatever you're searching for.

Start the Gesture Search app to begin a search. Use your finger to draw a big letter on the screen. After you draw a letter, search results appear on the screen. You can continue drawing more letters to refine the search or touch a search result.

Gesture Search can find contacts, music, apps, and bookmarks in the Browser app.

Google Finance

The Google Finance app is an excellent market-tracking tool for folks who are obsessed with the stock market or want to keep an eye on their portfolios. The app offers you an overview of the market and updates to your stocks as well as links to financial news.

To get the most from this app, configure Google Finance on the web, using your computer. You can create lists of stocks to watch, which is then instantly synchronized with your Galaxy Tab. You can visit Google Finance on the web at `www.google.com/finance`. As with other Google services, Google Finance is provided to you for free, as part of your Google account.

Google Sky Map

Ever look up into the night sky and say, "What the heck is that?" Unless it's a bird, an airplane, a satellite, or a UFO, the Google Sky Map can help you find what it is.

The Google Sky Map app is elegant. It basically turns the Galaxy Tab into a window you can look through to identify things in the night sky. Just start the app and hold the Galaxy Tab up to the sky. Pan the Tab to identify planets, stars, and constellations.

Avoiding Android viruses

How can you tell which apps are legitimate and which might be viruses or evil apps that do odd things to your phone? Well, you can't. In fact, most people can't, because most evil apps don't advertise themselves as such.

The key to knowing whether an app is evil is to look at what it does. If a simple grocery-list app uses the phone's text messaging service and the app doesn't need to send text messages, it's suspect.

In the history of the Android operating system, only a handful of malicious apps have been distributed, and most of them were found in Asia. Google routinely removes these apps from the Google Play Store, and a feature of the Android operating system even lets Google remove apps from your tablet. So, you're pretty safe.

Also, I highly recommend that you abstain from obtaining apps from anything but the official Google Play Store. The Amazon Market is okay, but some other markets are basically distribution points for illegal or infected software.

Movies

The Movies app is the Galaxy Tab's gateway to Hollywood. It lists currently running films and films that are opening, and it has links to your local theaters with showtimes and other information. The app is also tied into the popular Rotten Tomatoes website for reviews and feedback. If you enjoy going to the movies, you'll find the Movies app a valuable addition to your Galaxy Tab's app library.

SportsTap

I admit to not being a sports nut, so it's difficult for me to identify with the craving to have the latest scores, news, and schedules. The sports nuts in my life, however, tell me that the very best app for that purpose is a handy thing named SportsTap.

Rather than blather on about something I'm not into, just take my advice and obtain SportsTap. I believe you'll be thrilled.

TuneIn Radio

One of my favorite ways that the Galaxy Tab entertains me is as a little radio I keep by my workstation. I use the TuneIn Radio app to find a favorite Internet radio station, and then I sit back and work.

While TuneIn Radio is playing, you can do other things with your Tab, such as check Facebook or answer an e-mail. You can return to the TuneIn Radio app by choosing the triangle notification icon. Or just keep it going and enjoy the tunes.

Voice Recorder

The Galaxy Tab can record your voice or other sounds, and the Voice Recorder is a good app for performing this task. It has an elegant and simple interface: Touch the big Record button to start recording. Make a note for yourself or record a friend doing his Daffy Duck impression.

Previous recordings are stored in a list on the Voice Recorder's main screen. Each recording is shown with its title, the date and time of the recording, and the recording duration.

Zedge

The Zedge program is a helpful resource for finding wallpapers and ringtones — millions of them. It's a sharing app, so you can access wallpapers and ringtones created by other Android users as well as share your own. If you're looking for a specific sound or something special for Home screen wallpaper, Zedge is the best place to start your search.

Index

About the Author

Dan Gookin has been writing about technology for over 20 years. He combines his love of writing with his gizmo fascination to create books that are informative, entertaining, and not boring. Having written more than 120 titles with millions of copies in print translated into over 30 languages, Dan can attest that his method of crafting computer tomes seems to work.

Perhaps his most famous title is the original *DOS For Dummies,* published in 1991. It became the world's fastest-selling computer book, at one time moving more copies per week than the New York Times #1 bestseller (though as a reference, it could not be listed on the NYT Bestseller list). From that book spawned the entire line of *For Dummies* books, which remains a publishing phenomenon to this day.

Dan's most popular titles include *PCs For Dummies, Droid X For Dummies, Word For Dummies,* and *Laptops For Dummies.* He also maintains the vast and helpful website, www.wambooli.com.

Dan holds a degree in Communications/Visual Arts from the University of California, San Diego. Presently, he lives in the Pacific Northwest, where he enjoys spending time with his sons playing video games inside while they watch the gentle woods of Idaho.

Publisher's Acknowledgments

Senior Acquisitions Editor: Katie Mohr

Senior Project Editor: Kim Darosett

Editorial Assistant: Amanda Graham

Sr. Editorial Assistant: Cherie Case

Project Coordinator: Kristie Rees

Cover Photo: ©iStockphoto.com/ dmadig; Samsung Galaxy Tab 2 courtesy of Samsung

Apple & Mac

iPad For Dummies,
5th Edition
978-1-118-49823-1

iPhone 5
For Dummies,
6th Edition
978-1-118-35201-4

MacBook
For Dummies,
4th Edition
978-1-118-20920-2

OS X Mountain Lion
For Dummies
978-1-118-39418-2

Blogging & Social Media

Facebook
For Dummies
4th Edition
978-1-118-09562-1

Mom Blogging
For Dummies
978-1-118-03843-7

Pinterest
For Dummies
978-1-118-32800-2

WordPress
For Dummies,
5th Edition
978-1-118-38318-6

Business

Commodities
For Dummies,
2nd Edition
978-1-118-01687-9

Investing

Investing
For Dummies,
6th Edition
978-0-470-90545-6

Personal Finance
For Dummies,
7th Edition
978-1-118-11785-9

QuickBooks 2013
For Dummies
978-1-118-35641-8

Small Business
Marketing Kit
For Dummies,
3rd Edition
978-1-118-31183-7

Careers

Job Interviews
For Dummies,
4th Edition
978-1-118-11290-8

Job Searching with
Social Media
For Dummies
978-0-470-93072-4

Personal Branding
For Dummies
978-1-118-11792-7

Resumes
For Dummies,
6th Edition
978-0-470-87361-8

Success as a Mediator
For Dummies
978-1-118-07862-4

Diet & Nutrition

Belly Fat Diet
For Dummies
978-1-118-34585-6

Eating Clean
For Dummies
978-1-118-00013-7

Nutrition
For Dummies,
5th Edition
978-0-470-93231-5

Digital Photography

Digital Photography
For Dummies,
7th Edition
978-1-118-09203-3

Digital SLR Cameras
& Photography
For Dummies,
4th Edition
978-1-118-14489-3

Photoshop Elements 11
For Dummies
978-1-118-40821-6

Gardening

Herb Gardening
For Dummies,
2nd Edition
978-0-470-61778-6

Vegetable Gardening
For Dummies,
2nd Edition
978-0-470-49870-5

Health

Anti-Inflammation Diet
For Dummies
978-1-118-02381-5

Diabetes
For Dummies,
3rd Edition
978-0-470-27086-8

Living Paleo
For Dummies
978-1-118-29405-5

Hobbies

Beekeeping
For Dummies
978-0-470-43065-1

eBay For Dummies,
7th Edition
978-1-118-09806-6

Raising Chickens
For Dummies
978-0-470-46544-8

Wine For Dummies,
5th Edition
978-1-118-28872-6

Writing Young Adult
Fiction For Dummies
978-0-470-94954-2

Language & Foreign Language

500 Spanish Verbs
For Dummies
978-1-118-02382-2

English Grammar
For Dummies,
2nd Edition
978-0-470-54664-2

 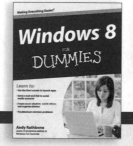  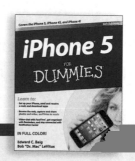

e Available in print and e-book formats.

French All-in One
For Dummies
978-1-118-22815-9

German Essentials
For Dummies
978-1-118-18422-6

Italian For Dummies,
2nd Edition
978-1-118-00465-4

Math & Science

Algebra I For
Dummies, 2nd Edition
978-0-470-55964-2

Anatomy and
Physiology For
Dummies, 2nd Edition
978-0-470-92326-9

Astronomy
For Dummies,
3rd Edition
978-1-118-37697-3

Biology For Dummies,
2nd Edition
978-0-470-59875-7

Chemistry
For Dummies,
2nd Edition
978-1-1180-0730-3

Pre-Algebra
Essentials
For Dummies
978-0-470-61838-7

Microsoft Office

Excel 2013
For Dummies
978-1-118-51012-4

Office 2013 All-in-One
For Dummies
978-1-118-51636-2

PowerPoint 2013
For Dummies
978-1-118-50253-2

Word 2013
For Dummies
978-1-118-49123-2

Music

Blues Harmonica
For Dummies
978-1-118-25269-7

Guitar For Dummies,
3rd Edition
978-1-118-11554-1

iPod & iTunes For
Dummies, 10th Edition
978-1-118-50864-0

Programming

Android Application
Development For
Dummies, 2nd Edition
978-1-118-38710-8

iOS 6 Application
Development
For Dummies
978-1-118-50880-0

Java For Dummies,
5th Edition
978-0-470-37173-2

Religion & Inspiration

The Bible
For Dummies
978-0-7645-5296-0

Buddhism For
Dummies, 2nd Edition
978-1-118-02379-2

Catholicism
For Dummies,
2nd Edition
978-1-118-07778-8

Self-Help & Relationships

Bipolar Disorder
For Dummies,
2nd Edition
978-1-118-33882-7

Meditation For
Dummies, 3rd Edition
978-1-118-29144-3

Seniors

Computers For
Seniors For Dummies,
3rd Edition
978-1-118-11553-4

iPad For Seniors
For Dummies,
5th Edition
978-1-118-49708-1

Social Security
For Dummies
978-1-118-20573-0

Smartphones & Tablets

Android Phones
For Dummies
978-1-118-16952-0

Kindle Fire HD
For Dummies
978-1-118-42223-6

NOOK HD
For Dummies,
Portable Edition
978-1-118-39498-4

Surface For Dummies
978-1-118-49634-3

Test Prep

ACT For Dummies,
5th Edition
978-1-118-01259-8

ASVAB For Dummies,
3rd Edition
978-0-470-63760-9

GRE For Dummies,
7th Edition
978-0-470-88921-3

Officer Candidate
Tests For Dummies
978-0-470-59876-4

Physician's Assistant
Exam For Dummies
978-1-118-11556-5

Series 7 Exam
For Dummies
978-0-470-09932-2

Windows 8

Windows 8
For Dummies
978-1-118-13461-0

Windows 8
For Dummies,
Book + DVD Bundle
978-1-118-27167-4

Windows 8 All-in-One
For Dummies
978-1-118-11920-4

 Available in print and e-book formats.

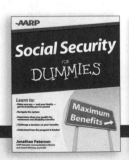

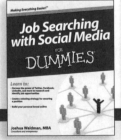